How to Produce, Perform and Write an Edinburgh Fringe Comedy Show

By Ian Fox

With contributions from Ashley Frieze

First published in 2012 by Ian Fox.

This edition in 2016 by Ian Fox

Copyright © 2016 Ian Fox

Photos © 2012 and © 2013 Ian Fox

The right of Ian Fox to be identified as the author of this work has been asserted by him in accordance with The 1988 Copyright, Designs and Patents Act. All rights reserved. No part of this publication may be reproduced, stored in a retrieval system, or transmitted, in any form or by any means, electronic, mechanical, photocopying, recording, or otherwise, without the prior permission of the author.

The reproduction of show descriptions from the 2010 and 2011 programmes is with kind permission from the Edinburgh Fringe Society who retain copyright of these descriptions.

www.ianfox.net

www.ashleyfrieze.co.uk

Cover design by Ian Fox.

ISBN-13: 978-1466438774

ISBN-10: 1466438770

ABOUT THE AUTHORS

Ian Fox is a stand-up comedian, writer and photographer from Cheshire. He first visited the Fringe in 2002 and accidentally produced his first show in 2003. Since then he's produced at least one show each year. In 2007 his solo show 'The Butterfly Effect' was commissioned by the BBC to be turned into a radio pilot.

Critics have described his Fringe shows as

"Funny fascinating and engaging" Kate Copstick – The Scotsman

"Fascinating, charming, intelligent and above all incredibly funny". Leeds Guide

"Succeeds admirably in being smart, funny and entertaining without a whiff of smugness". ★★★★ Julia Chamberlain – Chortle.co.uk

"A wonderfully entertaining hour" – ★★★★ British Comedy Guide

Ashley Frieze first visited and fell in love with the Fringe in 1994. He wrote, produced and performed his first full length show in 2004 – a comedy musical play simply called 'The Musical!' – described by the British Theatre Guide as *"endearingly gormless"*. He's been involved in show production every year since, and in 2010 developed his first solo stand-up show 'The Seven Deadly Sings'.

Critics have described his Fringe shows as:

"Witty, unpretentious and highly enjoyable slice of comedy theatre" – ★★★★ ThreeWeeks

"This charming show is the definition of warm, light-hearted entertainment" – ★★★★ Latest 7

"Great fun" – ★★★★ British Theatre Guide

ABOUT THE BOOK

This book shares fourteen years experience of producing shows at the Fringe for the price of a two café lattes and a muffin, without the social awkwardness of having to sit with the author in a coffee shop.

This guide is aimed at performers interested in producing their first shows at the Edinburgh Fringe. Highlighting the author's personal experiences of half-full houses, flat mates gone bad, hostel horror stories, campsite calamities, and general comedy cock-ups.

Although the author's background is in producing and performing stand-up comedy, the principles of venue hire, promotion and publicity are the same for shows of other genres, such as, sketch comedy, cabaret and theatre shows, as are the problems of managing large groups of performers.

The section on how to write shows details the author's approach to writing his shows as opposed to being a general how to write comedy guide.

This book is dedicated to all those who have made me laugh.

ACKNOWLEDGEMENTS

In helping me prepare this book I would like to thank the following for their cooperation:-

Ashley Frieze, Marissa Burgess, Seymour Mace, Lee Martin, The Mighty Swob, Carl Cooper, Mike Belgrave, Steve Bennett, Sarah Millican, Paul Sinha, Paul Harry Allan, Paul Kerensa, Lynn Ruth Miller, Bob Slayer, Imran Yusuf, Paul Sullivan, Josie Long, Robin Ince, Dan Willis, John Fleming, Dave Turquoise, David Longley, Danny Hurst, Eric Mutch, Chris Judge, Gill Smith, Spring Day, Bruce Fummey, Peter Michael Marino and The Edinburgh Fringe Festival Society.

I would also like to thank Alex Petty, Peter Buckley-Hill, Heidi and Andrew Waddington all of whom have helped me produce shows at the Fringe since 2003.

DISCLAIMER

Under UK Law business information contained in emails is subject to copyright law, therefore costs for some services are approximate and may vary on a client to client basis.

The performers mentioned by name in this book have all been contacted prior to publication and have consented for the stories they feature in to be included.

To protect the privacy of some individuals in some cases, pseudonyms have been used or names omitted entirely.

Contents

INTRODUCTION...15
WHAT IS A FRINGE SHOW?..15
BRIEF HISTORY OF THE FRINGE....................................16
WHO DOES FRINGE SHOWS?..18
WHAT KIND OF SHOWS GO TO THE FRINGE?..............18
WHY GO TO THE FRINGE?..18
WHO WATCHES FRINGE SHOWS?................................21
HOW PEOPLE WATCH FRINGE SHOWS........................21
HOW TO BOOK YOUR SHOW...22
WHERE TO START..22
CHOOSING THE RIGHT VENUE...23
STAND-UP AND SKETCH COMEDY VENUES.................23
OTHER VENUES..24
THEATRE SHOWS...25
TIMESLOT..25
DAYS OFF..25
VENUE HINTS AND TIPS...26
TURNAROUND TIME...26
STORAGE..27
HOW MUCH WILL IT COST?..28
WHO MAKES MONEY DURING THE FRINGE?..............28
FREE SHOW OVERHEADS...29
HOW MUCH WILL A PAID SHOW COST?..........................30
HOW MUCH DOES IT COST TO HIRE A VENUE?..........30
BOX OFFICE SPLIT WITH GUARANTEE TO VENUE........30
THE ABOVE CALCULATION IS NOT ACTUALLY
CORRECT...32
TICKET DEDUCTIONS..33
OUTRIGHT HIRE FEES...34
FREE TICKETS..34
IT'S EXPENSIVE...34
PAY WHAT YOU WANT (2013 ONWARDS)..........................34

THE CONVENTIONAL METHODS OF PROMOTING A FRINGE SHOW..................36
LIST IN THE FRINGE GUIDE..................36
BEST METHOD FOR WRITING THE 40 WORD BLURB...36
REGISTERING SHOW WITH THE FRINGE OFFICE........37
BLURB HINTS AND TIPS..................38
CHOOSING A FRINGE THUMBNAIL IMAGE..................38
IMAGE SELECTION HINTS AND TIPS..................41
DISCOUNT DEADLINE..................41
SAMPLE FRINGE PROGRAMME ENTRIES..................42
EXAMPLES OF BADLY WRITTEN BLURB..................44
BLURB HINTS AND TIPS..................46
COPYRIGHT OF 40 WORD BLURB..................46
ADVERT IN THE OFFICIAL FRINGE GUIDE..................47
FRINGE ADVERT HINTS AND TIPS..................47
PR PEOPLE..................47
PRESS RELEASE..................49
POSTERS IN VENUES AND ADDITIONAL LOCATIONS..51
FLYERS..................52
ADDITIONAL ADVERTISING..................53
THINKING OUTSIDE THE BOX..................54
Case Study: Tim Vine..................54
Case Study: Lewis Schaffer..................54
Case Study: Kunt And The Gang..................55
HOW TO KNOW IF WHAT YOU'VE DONE HAS WORKED
..................56
SO HOW DO YOU MAKE MONEY?..................56
FIND YOUR OWN PEOPLE..................57
DO YOUR OWN PR..................58
DON'T PAY FOR A VENUE..................58
DOES ANYONE MAKE MONEY ON THEIR SHOW?........58
CASE STUDY: COMIC A..................58
CASE STUDY: ASHLEY FRIEZE AND THE COSTS OF A FREE SHOW..................59
REGISTRATION FEES..................59

EQUIPMENT..60
PUBLICITY MATERIALS..60
PRODUCTION STAFF..60
PREVIEWS...60
SOMEWHERE TO LIVE..61
REVENUE..61
TOTAL COSTS..62
BOTTOM LINE..62
WHAT DID THE MONEY BUY ME?..............................62

PRE FRINGE PROMOTION..63

GET THE NAME OF YOUR SHOW RIGHT........................63
LIST IN THE FRINGE GUIDE – FREE SHOW SPECIFIC
ADVICE..64
PICNIC TICKETS..64

MARKETING MATERIALS...65

POSTERS...65
POSTER CONCEPTS...66
GET A DESIGNER..67
WHAT INFORMATION TO INCLUDE...............................67
POSTER HINTS AND TIPS..69
PHOTOSHOP LICENCE...69
THE BLACK BAR..69
PROOF READING PRINT OUTS.....................................70
COLOUR PROOFS..70
TECHNICAL SPECIFICATIONS......................................70
NOT AS PROFICIENT AS THEY THOUGHT....................72
PRINT ORDERS..72
FLYERS..72
PROMOTIONAL ITEMS...73

WHAT TO DO ONCE THE FESTIVAL STARTS................75

PLANNING TO DO STUFF WHILE YOU'RE THERE..........76
MANAGING YOUR SHOW..77
AUDIENCE SEATING PATTERNS..................................77

MAKE FRIENDS WITH THE OTHER SHOWS	78
KIDS	79
NON-ENGLISH SPEAKING AUDIENCES	80
TRANSPORTING PROPS	81
PROP TRANSPORTATION HINTS AND TIPS	81
PROP DISPOSAL	81
PROP HIRE AND PURCHASE	82
PROPS HINTS AND TIPS	82
PROS AND CONS OF HIRING EQUIPMENT	82
PROS AND CONS OF BUYING EQUIPMENT	83
UNWANTED VIDEO RECORDERS	83
FREE VENUE SPECIFIC SHOW MANAGEMENT	86
GET AN ASSISTANT	86
RUN-IN MUSIC	86
SHOW MANAGEMENT HINTS AND TIPS	87
TIMEKEEPING	87
FRONT OF HOUSE MANAGEMENT	88
LATECOMERS	89
DEALING WITH LATECOMERS: OPTION 1	90
DEALING WITH LATECOMERS: OPTION 2	91
CASE STUDY: FRIDAY NIGHT DRUNKS	91
COLLECTION SPEECH	92
VIOLENCE	93
FLYERING	94
THE ROYAL MILE	94
OUTSIDE YOUR VENUE	95
INSIDE YOUR VENUE	95
FLYERING HINTS AND TIPS	95
HOW TO FLYER	95
MAKE A SHOW OF YOURSELF	96
SCATTERGUN FLYERING	96
ONE TO ONE CONVERSATION	97
FLYERING ETIQUETTE	98
ANNOYING TACTICS	98
ASHLEY FRIEZE'S ADVICE	99

FLYERING HINTS AND TIPS...*100*
SPRING DAY'S FRINGE TIP...*101*
THE MOST IMPORTANT PIECE OF ADVICE FOR
SURVIVING THE FRINGE..102
ACCOMMODATION..102
HISTORY OF MY EDINBURGH ACCOMMODATION......104
2003..104
2004 and 2005..105
2006..106
2009..106
ACCOMMODATION HINTS AND TIPS...........................*107*
LESSONS LEARNT...109
FLAT SHARE HORROR STORIES..................................*110*
MISCELLANEOUS TRAVEL INFORMATION...................111
CAR...*111*
PARKING..111
TRAIN...*111*
AIR..*112*
COACHES..*112*
*CASH. HOW MUCH OF IT DO YOU NEED WHILE YOU'RE
THERE*...*113*
WHAT TO BRING WITH YOU..*114*
UNFORESEEN EXPENSES...*115*
FUN...*117*

WRITING AND PERFORMING SECTION........................118

THEMES...*118*
ROAD TESTING MATERIAL...*119*
DIRECTION...*119*
FORMATTING SHOWS...*120*
FORTY MINUTE LULL..*120*
LOCALISED REFERENCES...*121*
WORD PLAY...*121*
PRONUNCIATION...*122*
SWEARING..*123*

MULTIMEDIA..124
THE BUTTERFLY EFFECT – 2006..................................125
THE LORENZ STORY...126
LORENZ STORY WITH JOKES.......................................127
BUTTERFLY EFFECT FORMAT.....................................129
BUTTERFLY WRITING TIME..131
BUTTERFLY CONCLUSION...132
ONE MAN DEFECTIVE STORY......................................132
DEFECTIVE STORY FAILURES.....................................134
DEFECTIVE WRITING TIME...135
PAST REVIEWS...135
PREVIEW SHOWS..136
PREVIEW SHOW HINTS AND TIPS...............................138
 CRITICS AND REVIEWS...139
WHAT HAPPENS WHEN YOU GET GOOD OR BAD REVIEWS?..141
NOT GIVING OUT PRESS TICKETS..............................143
BADLY WRITTEN REVIEWS..143
WHY I DON'T READ MY REVIEWS................................145
WHY I DON'T THINK YOU SHOULD READ YOUR REVIEWS..147
WHAT IS A BAD SHOW?..149
WHAT MAKES A GOOD SHOW.....................................150

FRINGE TALES AND NIGHTMARES................................151

THE MIGHTY SWOB...151
DANNY HURST...156
ASHLEY FRIEZE...157

PERSONAL EXPERIENCES FROM THE FRINGE...........160

2003..160
EGOS..160
LESSONS LEARNT..161
2004..161
SOCIABLE DRINKERS...162
LACK OF TEAM WORK...163

EGOS AGAIN.. 163
BOUNCING CHEQUES.. 163
LESSONS LEARNT... 164
2005... 164
A CAD AND A BOUNDER.. 165
LESSONS LEARNT... 165
2006... 166
MORE RANDOM THAN YOU'RE EXPECTING............... 167
LESSONS LEARNT... 167
2007... 168
THE IVAN HOE... 168
WHEN STORIES ARE TOO PERSONAL...................... 169
BACKSTAGE BRAVADO.. 170
COMEDY IS A SERIOUS BUSINESS............................ 170
THE BIGGEST PROBLEM WITH ORGANISING GROUP SHOWS.. 171
LESSONS LEARNT... 172
2008... 172
ACCOMMODATION ISSUES AGAIN............................ 173
2009... 173
MONEY AGAIN... 173
2010... 174
AN AWARD WINNING PLAY.. 174
UNCOMFORTABLE BEYOND BELIEF......................... 176
EVERYONE LOVES A CAR WRECK............................ 177
2011... 177
NO IDEA HOW IT WORKS... 177
ONE FLYER TOO MANY... 177
YOU NEVER KNOW WHO'S IN THE CROWD............ 178
FINANCIAL PROBLEMS.. 179
BOB'S BOOKSHOP.. 179
WHAT DO THE AUDIENCE THINK?............................ 180
CONCLUSIONS.. 180
HAVE A SHOW... 180
LIFE AFTER THE FRINGE... 182

CLOSING POINTS	183
FINAL WORD	185
USEFUL RESOURCES	*185*
APPENDIX 1: PRODUCTION SCHEDULE FOR THE 2017 FRINGE	*186*
APPENDIX 2: ILLUSTRATIONS	*190*
APPENDIX 2: ILLUSTRATIONS	*191*

INTRODUCTION

I first visited the Edinburgh Fringe as a new comedian in 2002, staying for twelve nights, doing as many short spots as possible, and watching as many shows as I could. By the end of these twelve days I'd decided that, rather than be a spectator, I was going to return the following year in a show for the full run. At that point, I didn't know how to go about doing that.

I tried to get on stand-up showcases for new acts at the Fringe with no luck whatsoever. Then out of the blue a local event management company, who I'd done some gigs for, asked me if I wanted to produce a showcase for new acts in a venue they were running.

My first production – 'The Great Big Comedy Picnic' – started in 2003 and featured new acts from around the North West as well as guest appearances from more established acts, such as, Alan Carr and Jason Manford. Since 2003 I've produced at least one show at the Fringe each year in a range of different venues and formats, from my own one-man themed stand-up shows to compilation showcases. This guide is intended to share my experiences and to help performers new to the Fringe put on their own production successfully.

WHAT IS A FRINGE SHOW?

One definition of Fringe theatre is that it is performed without lavish sets, using minimal props and black material backgrounds. This approach was born out of simple necessity. Venues at the Edinburgh Fringe needed to programme as many shows as possible into a day and the only practical way to do this was to have as short a time as possible between one show finishing and the next one starting. With only a short changeover time, the outgoing show needs to clear the stage area as quickly as possible and get its audience to leave. The incoming show then needs to set the stage for their production and get its audience seated so the performance can start on time. Moving props and changing backdrops during this window was time consuming so productions reduced their stage set-ups. They would use the same black backgrounds and simply asked the audience to imagine they were watching people in a railway station, zoo or, ironically, a pub. I say ironically because a large number of venues at the Edinburgh Fringe are pubs and nightclubs turned into temporary theatre spaces for just over three weeks of the year.

Famous Fringe venues are created from buildings that for the rest of the year are universities, churches, nightclubs and sports halls. Temporary venues are created in tents and even moving buses have been utilised as performance spaces. In 2003 Alfie Joey used his own car to create the Fringe's smallest, and indeed cheapest, theatre space. The number of Fringe venues rises every year as the population of the Scottish capital find ever more creative ways to use anything with or without an address.

BRIEF HISTORY OF THE FRINGE

The Edinburgh International Festival was created in 1947 to enrich the cultural lives of people in the UK in the aftermath of World War Two. Eight theatre groups turned up uninvited to take part in the Festival that year and the trend continued for over ten years leading to the Festival Fringe Society being formed in 1959. In 1960 'Beyond the Fringe' with Peter Cook, Dudley Moore, Alan Bennett and Jonathan Miller premièred in Edinburgh tapping into the satire boom of the early 60s and helped establish the term Fringe in people's minds as the wildly successful show moved on to London's West End and Broadway. Ironically the show had actually been commissioned by the International Festival as a response to the newly emerging Fringe movement.

The birth of the Edinburgh Comedy Awards in 1981– still referred to by some as the Perrier Awards after the original sponsors, and the simultaneous rise of Alternative Comedy meant the Fringe started to feature more stand-up comedians in its programme. By the late 80s the Fringe had become a regular annual event for comedians, as winners of the comedy award gradually started to become household names – comedians and actors, such as, Stephen Fry, Hugh Laurie and Emma Thompson in the Cambridge Footlights, as well as Jeremy Hardy and Arnold Brown. In the 90s Frank Skinner, Steve Coogan, Lee Evans, Dylan Moran, Al Murray and The League of Gentlemen all won the main comedy award and the Fringe established itself as an essential part of the comedy calendar. Over time, the larger production companies moved in and the city's landlords, venue owners and council exploited every potential source of profit.

At the time of writing, the Fringe resembles the International Festival much more than the original bunch of gatecrashers who turned up uninvited in 1947. The largest arts festival in the world, the Fringe includes shows at Edinburgh Castle, EICC and televised comedy galas from the Festival Theatre. Performers signed with the large corporate agencies fill most of the premium venue spaces and the biggest selling shows usually involve household names holding chat shows or TV and film stars in well-established plays, such as, 'The Odd Couple', 'One Flew Over the Cuckoo's Nest' and 'Twelve Angry Men'.

Although various comedians had run free-entry shows over the years, 2005 saw free shows appearing in bigger numbers at the festival, since producing a free show proved to be more financially viable than paying the high rents charged to perform in the established venues. Some also believed that the strict programming policies of the main venues were preventing inexperienced or potentially unpredictable acts from putting on shows. The open to anyone policies of the free venues were embraced by critics at the festival, such as, Kate Copstick – reviewer for The Scotsman – as being in the true gatecrasher spirit of the Fringe. In 2016 the Fringe had over 3269 performances in its programme, 821 were free shows[1]. The biggest sections of the programme were comedy and theatre.

WHO DOES FRINGE SHOWS?

Over the years pretty much anyone has appeared on a Fringe stage; from Hollywood actors, corrupt former Conservative MPs, porn stars to anyone who has ever been on a stage on the comedy circuit. It's an international festival with performers from all over the world appearing. As for the comedians who go the Fringe you can expect to see everyone from brand new acts to TV regulars.

WHAT KIND OF SHOWS GO TO THE FRINGE?

The Fringe guide has sections for children's shows, cabaret, comedy, music, theatre, musical theatre and opera, physical theatre and dance. There isn't actually a miscellaneous section but over the years plenty of shows haven't quite fit into any one genre. In 2011 the Fringe office added the cabaret section to the guide in response to what was becoming a popular trend. Up to that point cabaret and burlesque shows had been listed in the comedy or theatre section. Anything goes at the Fringe, from shows with just one person and a microphone through to large ensemble casts in plays to Chinese acrobatic groups with pretty much everything in between.

WHY GO TO THE FRINGE?

For comedians the main two schools of thought on this are either to advance your comedy career or to get better as a comic. The first option aims to attract you more attention

---

[1] The actual number of free shows could have been in excess of 1000 due to a high number of PBH shows not listing in the official Fringe guide.

within the comedy industry, which might, hopefully, lead to picking up TV work or some kind of award. In some respects this first motivation makes sense, as faces from the Fringe guide published in June do start to appear on TV later in the year, on panel shows or as talking head interviews. However a Fringe show is a big financial risk and there is no guarantee that this will actually get you more work in the long run. There is a story that Hale and Pace performed to a small audience at the Fringe one day, just a handful of people, but one of that handful turned out to be a producer at London Weekend Television who went on to get them commissioned for a TV series. Whilst this story makes interesting reading I can assure you that there are plenty of comics who do shows at the Fringe to a similarly small number without anyone in the crowd having anything to do with TV casting or production. Much like the magazines Chat and Take a Break, which always seem to run stories about readers who entered their competitions for years and then finally won one of the prizes, you have to remember that there are lots of other people who enter their competitions for years and win bugger all.

For every Hale and Pace story, I can think of numerous others who ended up getting themselves in debt paying for a Fringe show and then struggled to pay it off for years afterwards, not reaping any obvious benefit from the experience at all. Their stories aren't quite so interesting or widely circulated because they lack that big finish. The reality of the Fringe is that this idea some people have about going up there to "really go for it this year and try and get my face seen" is effectively gambling, with really poor odds. There is no guarantee that the right people will come and see your show, and looking through old copies of the Fringe guide I quite often see names and faces and wonder "whatever happened to them?"

There are industry people in Edinburgh in August, without doubt. In 2010 I found myself in conversation with someone I'd met ten minutes earlier and discovered that they were a producer for a well-known TV production company – this kind of thing does happen at Fringe – and during the course of our chat the shows they were going to watch came up. Browsing through their methodically written out schedule I noticed that there wasn't a single performer on the list who wasn't already on TV. Industry types are frequently looking to consolidate what they already have, rather than discover something new and unheard of. Aiming for fame and fortune in a three week period in August is an unrealistic aim, which is why most performers who I know, who go to the Fringe, do it for reason number two – the Fringe is a unique opportunity to develop your act and hone your performance skills.

The performers that treat the experience as a boot camp for comedians, using the opportunity to perform every day up to a handful of times a day, are the ones who usually return year after year feeling like they've gained something from the experience each time. Stand-up comedy in the UK is different to that in the US where comics can perform every day. After a twenty five day run at the Fringe you're more confident as a performer and feel the benefit of so much stage time in a short period when you return to the circuit in September. August is also a difficult time to get gigs on the comedy circuit with a lot of clubs taking the summer off, which is another reason the Fringe became popular with comedians as it seemed like a chance to earn money, or at least perform regularly, in an otherwise slow month of the year.

The key to a successful Fringe is to set a realistic target for yourself. Take an idea you want to explore and see if you can turn it into an hour long show, find others whom you can create a showcase with so you can practice doing a decent ten or twenty minute set or simply go up there to have some fun. Many performers find that watching a lot of the more established acts in a short space of time teaches them a lot about the art of comedy.

There is also a benefit to writers staging productions of their own plays. Some bursary schemes run by the BBC and other organisations only accept applications from writers who have written a script that has actually been produced. The experience of working with performers gives more insight into how scriptwriters and actors work together and how audiences respond to material. The Fringe is a great opportunity to test drive a project and thus qualify for such schemes.

WHO WATCHES FRINGE SHOWS?

Audiences at the Fringe are from varying backgrounds. A recent survey listed a majority of them as Scottish and from Edinburgh, Glasgow and surrounding areas. These audience members visit shows at the weekend and in the evenings throughout the festival. Audiences from elsewhere, such as, England, Wales and Ireland come up on holiday and visit from a few days to a week; the cost of accommodation tends to prohibit them from staying longer. The holiday audiences watch shows all through the day as well as in the evenings. A smaller section of the audience are English speaking visitors from Australia, the US and Canada, again watching shows all through the day and evening. A minority of audiences are non-English speaking from mainland Europe or Japan.

HOW PEOPLE WATCH FRINGE SHOWS

Audiences at the Fringe rarely watch one show and usually try to see as many as possible. Often they'll visit one venue or area with a number of venues in it so they can easily get from one show to another, usually within a very short period of time. They're conscious of time and apprehensive about shows starting late or overrunning. Tickets for paid for shows are usually purchased in advance and the tickets are collected from either the Fringe box office on the High Street, the Half Price Hut on the Mound or the University of Edinburgh Information Centre. The experienced Fringe-goer orders their tickets from the venue box office and collects them there where the queues are shorter; or buys their tickets online for collection at a kiosk, which prints them within a few seconds and has a very short queue.

Since the increase in free shows in 2005, Fringe-goers with time to spare in between paid shows will see what's on at a nearby free venue in order to pack more shows into their day, often making their decision at the last minute, with varying reasons for choosing a show based on timing, or face to face contact with performers.

HOW TO BOOK YOUR SHOW

WHERE TO START

Firstly you need to find a venue and book yourself in. Start with the participants section on edfringe.com. The Fringe guide to choosing a venue contains a list of all performance spaces along with basic information, such as, location, capacity, technical specifications and health and safety requirements. Basic equipment usually includes a PA system and stage lighting, but assume nothing. Some venues are very basic indeed. Other things, such as, projectors, screens and DVD players may be included by the higher-end venues, but if you need to provide your own you will need to think carefully about installation and storage.

Another practical consideration is the storage and movement of any props or equipment you need for your show. The Fringe ideal is to travel light, but even the most cut down of theatre or music performances still have plenty of objects to get into position for show time. You should be looking at whether your venue has storage space, dressing rooms if you need them and how near these are to the performance space. Performers who have to carry heavy bags to and from their venue every day for three weeks soon lose their enthusiasm.

Make initial contact with the venues via email. You will need to give them a working title for your show along with a written description and breakdown of it. Venues don't want to programme bad shows for artistic and commercial reasons; you might think your idea of 'Fred West: The Musical' might be hilarious but they might not agree. For this reason some venues may require you to supply videos of performances and other supporting pieces of material, such as, scripts and reviews. The more professional you make these, the better your chance of being included in the venue's programme. The paid venues have more applications than they accept so you should apply to plenty of venues.

CHOOSING THE RIGHT VENUE

STAND-UP AND SKETCH COMEDY VENUES

The Pleasance, The Stand and Assembly are all excellent venues for comedy but you will need to have proven track record to be considered for these venues since they try to maintain a solid brand name for good quality comedy. They're frequently oversubscribed with applications and it's unlikely for a complete newcomer to be given an offer.

Gilded Balloon, Underbelly and Just The Tonic are more open to newcomers, but they might not commit to renting a specific space until very late on. This means you might get a yes from them but not until the day before the deadline for registering for shows.

Sweet, C-Venues and The Space tend to focus on theatrical productions, though they will accept comedians. They don't appear to be too discerning when it comes to the quality of comedy shows and thus have a chequered reputation among the critics. One critic told me that they never hold out much hope when sent to review comedy in these venues.

The best advice is to do your research. Staging your show in completely the wrong venue is possibly worse than not staging it at all. If in doubt about the suitability of a venue, ask other people who have performed there. The larger venues are unlikely to negotiate on hire fees for newer acts, putting all the financial risks for these shows on the producers rather than the venue and this is worth knowing up front – for a very high profile venue you might have to plan a business model based on making a huge loss.

The Laughing Horse Free Festival and Peter Buckley-Hill's Free Fringe are very accessible to newcomers and much lower risk financially. PBH tries to vet acts before giving them a space, so it might be worth your time to travel somewhere so he or a close colleague can see you perform. At present the Free Festival doesn't have any explicit vetting procedures in place, though being known to the Laughing Horse organisers from other gigs can help get a better slot.

OTHER VENUES

There are other spaces available for hire in Edinburgh but not many of them are that noticeable when it comes to comedy. They might be easier to get into but if the audience that frequents them are more interested in theatre it's going to make it difficult to get the right people in to watch the show.

There isn't just one Fringe audience. There are many sub-groups of people looking for different types of shows with expectations set by the perceived standards and style of each venue. Choosing a venue that reflects your audience can make a big difference to the box office figures and the atmosphere of your show.

THEATRE SHOWS

C-Venues, Sweet, The Space and other independents are more suited to theatre shows. Each of them will vary in the amount of equipment and lighting they have on hand. The main consideration for picking a venue should be the location. If you're unfamiliar with the geography of Edinburgh my advice would be to check a venue map and find somewhere that is a short distance from a concentration of big venues. Some venues, although excellent spaces, are simply too far out of town for Fringe audiences. Often on a schedule, the average Fringe-goer will be reluctant to spend extra time and money getting to an out of the way venue.

TIMESLOT

Shows earlier in the day are more likely to get press reviews as there isn't as much competition to get reviewers in but shows later in the day are more likely to get punters in. If you're on your own and want reviews it's worth thinking about going early in the day. If you're in a compilation show, then later is better.

If your show is scheduled after 9pm the chances are that you'll get a boozier crowd, so make sure it's suitable. Compilation stand-up shows are good in those slots or anything crude, rude or adult themed. A one man play about the struggles of a Catholic priest probably isn't great for 11.30pm slot in a nightclub on a Saturday night, for instance, but the bawdy 'Shaggers', which promises stand-up comedy about sexual themes easily pulls in anyone with a drink in their hand.

DAYS OFF

Most shows have a day off. If you're in a compilation you have the advantage of being able to take a day off, either to rest, or simply see a show on at the same time as you, without affecting your revenue from collections or ticket sales, as the show can still go ahead without you.

If you're on your own stick to just one day off in the middle of the festival – the middle Tuesday is most common.

VENUE HINTS AND TIPS

* Be wary of venues that aren't organised enough to have diagrams of performance spaces and technical breakdowns. We're only talking about a pen and paper drawing of how the room is going to be laid out and a list of their equipment. If they can't get that organised in January, what will they be like in August?

* Be wary of venues that take an unreasonable amount of time to reply to correspondence. A couple of days is reasonable to expect a reply to an email. Again either their organisational skills are questionable or you're low on their list of priorities. These things can indicate potential problems later on.

TURNAROUND TIME

Check how much time you have between the previous performance ending and your show starting; and your show ending and the next show starting. Anything less than 15 minutes is likely to be problematic and stressful. If time is tight, then ask about the type of show you're following or preceding. For example, two solo stand-up acts with no props have almost no set-up so can tolerate a quicker change-over, compared to two 20-man sketch shows with almost unlimited props and sketches where they shower the audience with confetti that needs to be swept up.

STORAGE

Not all venues have the necessary storage space for props and other items you might need for your show. Free venues usually don't have any storage space at all. Paid venues will have storage but it still might not be suitable. For example, in 2003 a magician I was working with decided that he couldn't store props in the Underbelly due to the venue being too damp. Dampness is an issue at the Underbelly and the Caves venues on Cowgate. During show runs in the Caves the technicians have to install plastic tents over the sound and lighting desks to prevent condensation from dripping into the equipment.

Storage space is usually available at the Pleasance, Gilded Balloon and Assembly venues as well as some C-Venues, Sweet and The Space. However these spaces can't guarantee security. Keeping your props with you might be the best option if you are using computers or other expensive items.

HOW MUCH WILL IT COST?

The first thing anyone usually tells you is they lost money on their show. This might seem surprising that year after year people are going up there to lose money. There are some theories as to why people keep doing it. My theory is that for a self-employed comic making a decent amount a year, paying for a Fringe show is simply more fun than giving it to the tax man. This would account for some comics' year on year return to the Fringe.

WHO MAKES MONEY DURING THE FRINGE?

Edinburgh City Council for one. Landlords another. Venues most definitely, both on their performance spaces and bars and the increase in trade is great for the other bars, clubs and restaurants in the city. Edinburgh's hotels certainly put their prices up and enjoy a high occupancy rate. Production companies that promote Fringe shows make a large percentage of their yearly profit in August.
As for performers, some of them do actually make money, particularly the savvy ones. There are certain things however that you can't get out of paying for.

One option for keeping your Fringe costs down is simply to move to Scotland, that way you're not paying the extortionate rents for a holiday let in Edinburgh. I personally doubt that many of the local performers are losing money on their shows, particularly the ones appearing in the Free Festival, PBH Free Fringe and The Stand comedy club.

FREE SHOW OVERHEADS

Free shows have the simplest overheads to calculate because they aren't complicated by taxes and venue guarantee percentages, so we'll cover them first.

Fringe entry fee is usually around £295[2], £90 entry fee in the Free Festival booklet, or for PBH's Free Fringe in 2016 there was a voluntary contribution of £3 per show or £5 per show for rooms holding over 100 people. Accommodation costs around £600[3], living expenses – based on £12 per day and 26 days in Edinburgh – £312, posters and flyers £120. Then there's travel to the Fringe and any additional expenses you might incur. Adding this up comes to an estimated cost of £1500 for a full run.

To this you must add all the costs of living normally back home. Rent, credit card payments, bills, direct debits and council tax must still be paid. Comedian Mike Belgrave told me *"I put all my expenses into a spread sheet around about January. I go back to it sporadically and add and subtract various costs. I'm also able to see where I'm unnecessarily spending and start making cuts. Putting aside 10% of your earnings as soon as you can alleviates the costs. It also makes you aware of how much you need closer to August so you'll automatically try and tighten your belt. Whatever you do avoid putting it on credit cards."*

A full case study of a Free Festival show is included later.

---

[2] It's been below £300 since 2003.

[3] Based on sharing a room in centrally located flat.

HOW MUCH WILL A PAID SHOW COST?

It's all dependent on what you decide to buy into. A quick answer is £7000 – that's easily what you could pay up front and what you'd stand to lose if your show is a total write-off. If you're looking at paid venues the first thing you need to learn before you go any further is how to use a speadsheet.[4]

Tell some people you're planning on coming to the Fringe and they will just assume you are made of money. Advertising sales agents see naïve first time Fringe producers as a big bag of money walking in through the door. Adverts that only cost £50 here and £50 there soon mount up. Flyering and poster distribution services can be very expensive and your venue may be creative in finding services to charge you for that you didn't know you needed, or had signed up to pay for.

It's not that people are trying to rip you off. A temporary economy springs up in August in Edinburgh involving workers who need paying and equipment that needs hiring – someone has to fund it and the producers and performers are the first port of call.

HOW MUCH DOES IT COST TO HIRE A VENUE?

Different venues obviously have different costs. The two most common ways of doing it are the box office split with guarantee or outright venue hire.

BOX OFFICE SPLIT WITH GUARANTEE TO VENUE

The most common method for renting a space is the box office split deal with 40% of ticket revenue going to the venue. However you have to guarantee that the venue will

---

[4] Excel or Google sheets are both good options.

receive a minimum fee for rental and pay them this at the time of booking the space.

The minimum fee is a percentage of the total possible box office revenue. As an example a 50 seat venue with 25 shows has 1250 tickets for sale. If the average ticket price is £8, the possible total box office is 1250 tickets, multiplied by £8 which equals £10,000. The box office split on a total sell out will be 40% of this figure, £4000 – however the hire fee will be subject to VAT – an extra £800. At the time of booking the venue will ask you to pay 40% of their £4000 possible box office revenue – £1920 inclusive of VAT. Or to put it another way 16% of the maximum potential box office takings plus VAT.

Once the festival is over the venue looks at what your total box office takings were and calculates 40% of that as their cut. Let's say you averaged 25 full price tickets per show. You total box office takings would be £5000. The venue's 40% cut would be £2000 plus VAT. Total fee payable £2400, you have already paid £1920 when you booked the room, so you would owe the venue £280, which the venue will issue an invoice for and remove from your box office account.

If you only sold 15 tickets per show, total box office would be £3000, the venue's 40% cut would be £1200 plus VAT. You've already paid them £1920 so you don't owe them anything, but since your £1920 was a guaranteed minimum fee they don't owe you anything either.

However the venue expenses don't stop at rental, usually there is compulsory fee for inclusion in the venue brochure, usually around £600 excluding VAT. It's probably a bad thing to be missing from these programmes, as they're part of how the large venues work towards getting people through the door of your show, but be wise to it before you sign up. Be realistic about how much your show will cost you up front and how much you stand to lose or gain if you do not get your expected audience numbers through the doors.

Many shows will get audiences that are in double figures and fluctuate from the teens to mid-twenties. If you're expecting to sell the show out, then it should be because you already have a following; or have amazing plans for promoting the show to the public.

Approximate up front cost of venue £2800

Next you have to register the show with the Fringe office and be included in the programme. Do this before the discount deadline and you can save about £100.

Fringe Entry £300

Total compulsory payments **£3100,** excluding cost of printed material, such as, posters and flyers. Add the cost of someone to hand out the damn bits of paper for you and the roof over your head for the month, plus food, drink, and travel to Scotland.

A quick calculation based on tickets being £8 each means you have to sell 388 tickets over the run to get those expenses back. Based on 25 shows that is 16 full price tickets per show in a 50 seat room to break even.

Does that seem likely on a first time run to you?

THE ABOVE CALCULATION IS NOT ACTUALLY CORRECT

The £8 ticket price mentioned in the sum was actually just for convenience. There will be deductions on every ticket sold before the money reaches you, which you need to understand before you book the space.

TICKET DEDUCTIONS

Firstly VAT is one expense often forgotten about. VAT is payable on the ticket price so for every £8 ticket you only receive £6.40 – current UK rate 20%.

Tickets sold through the Fringe office are subject to 6% commission fee plus VAT. An £8 ticket sold through the Fringe office is equal to £5.94. A condition of listing the show in the Fringe guide is that you allocate a minimum of 25% of your available tickets to the Fringe box office. Many people prefer to order tickets through the Fringe office so you might well add to that figure as you go along.

For tickets bought at the venue deductions on your ticket revenue will be VAT, plus a bank fee for anyone who used a card to pay for the ticket – which is most people. Card fees are usually between 2% to 4% of the total ticket price. Then there is the actual ticket itself. Venues charge you for the paper and ink used to make the ticket, up to 20p each.

A £8 ticket bought at the venue could be equal to just £5.88 in your box office fund.

If we do the calculation again with the correct figures total venue hire of £3100 you actually have to sell 527 tickets to break even. Based on 25 shows that is 21 full price tickets per show in a 50 seat room to break even – but then you haven't bought any advertising material yet.

This assumes you get full price for the ticket. The half price hut is a big ticket seller and you only get half the ticket price, less costs. You are also advised to run 'two for one' offers to simply get a larger audience number in. Plus you can forget about selling a lot of tickets in preview week, most shows have to give tickets away for free to get an audience in.

OUTRIGHT HIRE FEES

Other venues will charge a flat fee to hire a space – approximately £1800 plus VAT – allowing you to keep all your box office takings. These venues will still make the same deductions, such as, VAT, Fringe commission, bank card fees and ticket printing before the ticket money reaches you. They may also have clauses in the contract that limit the amount of free tickets you can give away or discount in price.

FREE TICKETS

If you decide to give out free tickets to your show the venue may still charge you for them, effectively charging you their 40% cut of the ticket price.

IT'S EXPENSIVE

You can spend a lot of money on getting the right venue and paying for the services that they consider compulsory – that's fixed before you've even considered the costs of printed promotional material and PR.

PAY WHAT YOU WANT (2013 onwards)

The 'Pay-What-You-Want' model is still a fairly limited option when it comes to producing shows as it's only available at a few venues. Essentially it's a crossover between a paid and a free show.

Originating from Bob Slayer's shows in The Hive – and his subsequent pop-up venues – 'Pay-What-You-Want' shows offer tickets for sale in advance for £5 to guarantee entry into shows. They also offer a collection bucket at the end for those that hadn't bought tickets. This business model proved successful for bigger name acts who had previously been uncomfortable with the idea of doing a free show and then asking for a contribution at the end.

For performers with an established Fringe reputation, such as, Ivan Brackenberry and Phil Kay it's understandable why they're attracted to the system, it gives them a lump-sum payout from the Fringe office in late September, as well as giving them cash each day during the festival. It also distances them from the Free shows which are routinely criticised for not exercising quality control on their shows.

Since then this model has been adopted by the both Just the Tonic – who ran this model in 2015 and 2016 – and the Gilded Balloon who ran an entire separate venue in 2016 based on this system – we're waiting to see if they'll do it again in 2017.

At Just the Tonic 'PWYW' spaces are rented and paid for in advance. Prices are negotiable dependent on room size and time of day. One teatime show in a 60 seater quoted me a total rent of £2300 with £1150 payable upfront. The outstanding balance being taken from box office revenue and bucket contributions. An earlier daytime show quoted £1200 and a midnight show £1000.

The fees get you access to box office staff, ushers to bring in audience members and block latecomers. They also get access to a decent technical set-up and with better levels of equipment found in the free venues with more controllable lighting, and a guarantee that equipment will work. However additional fees for technical staff to operate sound and lighting desks will be charged usually around £300 for a full run and is payable on final settlement in October.

Overall better facilities than a free show and cheaper than a premium venue. Downside is sometimes it's harder to get people into these shows than in free venues.

THE CONVENTIONAL METHODS OF PROMOTING A FRINGE SHOW

Once you've booked a venue you are going to have to promote the show and get audiences in.

LIST IN THE FRINGE GUIDE

You get 40 words to describe your show in the Fringe guide. People complain it's not enough space to fully get your message across. I think it's fine if you just think about it and spend some time editing it – that's exactly 40 words.

To quote an audience member who was kind enough to supply feedback on the shows they had watched at the Fringe in 2010 *"if you can't sum up your show in a few words, I get the feeling you don't know what you're doing."* The Fringe programme is the most important piece of advertising for your show. It's a huge market of potential audience members interested in watching shows and all you have to do is write something to persuade them to come along. *If it were impossible to say something meaningful in 40 words then Twitter would surely never have caught on. If it's good enough for Stephen Fry, a Fringe regular of the 80s, then it's good enough for any Fringe act* – another 40 words.

BEST METHOD FOR WRITING THE 40 WORD BLURB

Before you write anything create a list of the elements that you think will help sell the show including a concise description of what the show is and what it's about, useful press quotes if you have any and if it's a comedy show something funny.

Test market 'the funny' on friends and family to see that you get the correct response. I usually write out blurb on paper and then watch them as they read it. If they laugh you've done it right. Once you've decided on these key elements start assembling things into a clear statement.

When you have the first draft of your blurb see how many words you have, then take another pass at it looking for unnecessary repetition. Use combining words to cut the word count and then keep taking a pass at your show description making adjustments until you reach the magic number. Always read your description out loud to check that it sounds right and make sure you leave enough time so as you can sleep on it and then look at it again the following day to see if you still like it. Bear in mind that the 40 word description also includes your show title. For the 'The Great Big Comedy Picnic – Free' I actually get 34 words to describe the show and 'Ian Fox Exposes Himself – Free' I get 35 words to describe the show.

REGISTERING SHOW WITH THE FRINGE OFFICE

Show submissions to the Fringe office are done through the participants section of the edfringe.com website. Once registered you can enter shows into the programme using the automated system, which allows you to save your progress and make changes before final submission. The online system gives you an exact word count and won't let you list anything over the 40 word limit.

In the past I know people who have tried hyphenating words to trick the software, only to receive a phone call from the Fringe office informing them they've gone over the word count and need to do it again. The Fringe office checks every listing so don't waste time trying to trick the system – it won't work. Shows can also be registered by fax or post.

Shortly after registering your show the Fringe office will send you a proofing copy of your show's entry in the programme for you to check that all details are correct.

They will give you a small amount of time if you need to change anything.

BLURB HINTS AND TIPS

* If you're doing a free show it is helpful to include the word 'free' at the end of the show title; it might cost you a word but it'll get a healthy flow of freeloaders drifting in once the festival starts. You don't need to repeat the word free in the blurb.

* It's helpful to include positive press comments from respectable publications. Comments you've submitted yourself to a website using a fake name, for example, "genius" (www.fakequotes.com) doesn't fool anyone and can put punters off. If you don't have decent press just write more funny stuff.

Speaking of 'genius,' if you're promoting a comedy show then here's one small piece of advice: don't use the word 'genius' in your blurb. It's the most overused term in comedy. A search of the website ComedyCV.co.uk reveals shows there are currently 92 'geniuses' using the word 'genius' on their CV. However, if you happen to be an actual genius, such as, a professor of particle physics or if you can do a Rubik's cube in under 2 minutes using just your knob, then it's a very good idea to mention that. If you're just telling jokes and saying funny things then show everyone how unique a comic talent you are by finding a better and more original way to describe yourself.

CHOOSING A FRINGE THUMBNAIL IMAGE

The 2010 Fringe programme was radically different from previous years as it was the first to include an image for every show. Some shows benefited from this and others didn't take full advantage of it. The biggest difference is that it radically altered the timetable for producing artwork. Previously I used to create the show artwork in July. To include an image with your listing you need to have an image file with the Fringe office in April.

Looking at the programmes from 2010 and 2011 there were a few different approaches to choosing an image.

Option 1. A small version of the poster image.

This is probably the best option if you've got an advert in the programme but not massively necessary if you're only planning on having a campaign based on posters and flyers. The main objective should still be an eye catching image. Poster images do not always scale down to thumbnail size well enough to be effective.

Option 2. A professional promo shot of the performer.

This is a safe bet. It gives the show an air of professionalism but possibly isn't as effective as options 1, 3 and 4. The main advantage of this is that it gives you the option of delaying the creation of your posters until after the Fringe guide comes out.

Option 3. A professionally shot image of the performer live on stage.

This also works well, gives the show an air of professionalism and defers the deadline for creating the poster. It tends to be used more by theatre productions but can work well with stand-up.

Option 4. An image of something in keeping with the show title and theme that neither depicts the performer nor the show's primary artwork.

I think this option works really well and shows your audience some 'out of the box' thinking. It can certainly create a unique selling point for your show. An example from the past includes one-liner comedian Gary Delaney's

'No Whimsy' road sign logo indicating that his show was made up entirely of jokes with punchlines, rather than stories about badgers.

If you want to include an image that is representative of your show then a photo library should have something of interest. You can get cheap high resolution print images from iStockphoto. You can also try the photo sharing site Flickr. Make sure you contact the owner of any image you select in order to get permission to use it. Photographers own the copyright of any image they take.

Option 5. A placeholder image using the Free Festival or PBH Free Fringe logo.

This is convenient and helps to give the free shows branding. The downside is that your show loses its unique identity as numerous other shows have the same image. It's better to put some time and thought into it in April rather than be annoyed with yourself in June when the programme comes out and you fail to spot your own show on the page.

Option 6. A logo or graphic representation of the show.

This is also a good choice. Image files don't have to be a photo; they can be a graphic image or logo fitting your show. An example from the 2011 guide is a show called 'Spaghetti Lolognaise' that used a parody of a spaghetti sauce label as it's image. Another example is the cartoon drawing of two pandas shagging used by the show 'Shaggers.'

Option 7. A cartoon or illustration of the performer.

I think this also works, funny drawings fit in the small space quite well.

Option 8. Amateurish home-made images.

I'm not going to single any shows out, but if you look through old programmes it's obvious which shows are letting themselves down and it's usually the self-produced shows. The paid venues insist on you having high quality artwork. Image makes a difference when it comes to marketing a show. Spend time finding a great image rather than something shot on your phone or from the back row of a pub gig. It's in your interest.

IMAGE SELECTION HINTS AND TIPS

The size of the image in the programme is quite small so bear that in mind when cropping images to fit the 29mm square. You need to be close in on the subject with no wasted space around them. It's worth getting a printout of the image at actual size to see if the print version works before you send it to the Fringe office. Computer screens can be quite deceptive as images often appear brighter and more vivid than they will appear on paper. Images on screen can also appear bigger than actual print size.

Free photo editing for basic tasks like cropping can be done on cloud computing sites, such as, photoshop.com and with free tools, such as, Google's Picasa. Full colour print outs can be done in any high street photo shop for around 30p each. You should be able to fit 6 shots on to one 6×4 inch print, which means it's an incredibly cost effective way of road testing your artwork.

DISCOUNT DEADLINE

Just a reminder that there is a discount for listing a show in the Fringe programme three weeks before the main deadline closes. Check the edfringe.com site for the timetable. You are still able to edit your programme description and change the supplied image up to the final deadline at no extra cost. This is definitely worth doing. The money saved can be put to a better use during the Fringe.

SAMPLE FRINGE PROGRAMME ENTRIES

You can download full versions of past Fringe programmes in PDF format from various websites. Have a look through them to see how shows list themselves. Look out for shows similar to the one you're thinking of producing and see how they went about selling themselves.

I think these shows are good examples of well written blurb. Clearly time and effort has been spent making use of each word.

Sarah Millican – Chatterbox

Sarah's only criticism at school was that she was a chatterbox. Still is. Now it's her job. She hopes the same fate didn't befall the school bike. www.sarahmillican.co.uk

The Lost Letters of Cathy G

In a junk shop I stumbled across a wad of letters forgotten since the 1960s. Mixing stand-up with storytelling, I'll blow dust off these tales of love struck boyfriends and hopeful groupies. http://paulharryallen.weebly.com/

Paul Sinha – Extreme Anti White Vitriol

Paul Sinha has been described as a gay man, doctor, quizzer, bachelor, acclaimed comedian and racist. This year he'd like to deny one of those, while adding new labels of his own. 'Truly wonderful' (Scotsman).

Paul Kerensa – Borderline Racist

Dutchmen think Germans are bicycle-thieves... Latvians swear in Russian... Finns: introverted sauna-lovers... 'British Comedy Award' nominee (writer: 'Not Going Out', 'Miranda', 'Now Show') uncovers every nation's thoughts on their neighbours. **** (Metro). 'Wildly talented' (Chortle). www.paulkerensa.com

Josie Long – Be Honourable

Josie presents a ramshackle call to arms. Come, or she'll find you and cut your face up real good. She's 5'5". Every show she's done has received 2,3,4 and 5* reviews, so she must be doing something.

Aaaaaaaaaaaaaaaaaaaarghh! It's the Malcolm Hardee Comedy Punch Up Debates – and they're Free

Top comedy names. Two Debates. Monday "Comedians are psychopathic masochists with a death wish". Tuesday "Racist or sexist jokes?" It doesn't matter if they're funny!

Lynn Ruth Miller – Granny's Gone Wild

Lynn Ruth Miller, the world's oldest cougar, is 77! She raps, she jokes – she's gone mad. Her show is comedy at its worst – outrageous proof that when body parts drop to your ankles they can still swing.

Bob Slayer – Punk Rock Chat show

Wild liberating banter, games and stories from a rock'n'roll tour manager who has travelled the world with Stooges, Electric Eel Shock, Bloodhound Gang etc. Punk rock comedy: no rules, no limits, no refunds! www.bobslayer.com

Robin Ince Asks Why? – Free

Troubled youth in middle-age returns with new queries about existence and other problems. 'Grade A bile ... great hour by a great comedian' (Scotsman). 'Intellectually audacious' (Evening Standard). May contain Belle and Sebastian references.

Imran Yusuf – An Audience with Imran Yusuf

The fast talking lyrical machine-gun comic slows it down for a deep and meaningful look at life with personal stories and a unique life philosophy. www.imranyusuf.com

Dan Willis – Michael Jackson World's Greatest Entertainer

Can Willis prove that Michael Jackson is truly the world's greatest entertainer? A celebration of the music and moves, with a few laughs along the way. Suitable for all ages. **** (List). **** (ThreeWeeks).

EXAMPLES OF BADLY WRITTEN BLURB

Rather than single out people for making tiny mistakes when they listed their show in the Fringe guide, I've put together this fake list of show descriptions inspired by examples from recent Fringe guides. On first view they look like reasonable show descriptions but the authors could have saved themselves a few words by carefully choosing different ones.

Spanking The Monkey

<u>Brice Smith and Smiling Goat Comedy present</u> a <u>storytelling</u> show about the pressures we put on ourselves and each other. <u>Written and performed by Brice Smith</u>

Firstly there is some unnecessary repetition going on. The performer name and comedy company are listed in the company details under the show title. In any case I doubt anyone from the Smiling Goat is actually in the show, so their name could have been dropped from the description – saving 4 words. Secondly in the genre guide located at the bottom of the show details next to the dateline, it's down as "storytelling" so that's repetition – saving 1 word. Finally a "written by" credit might well be nice but this is advertising we're talking about and it's not helping to sell the show. You can put credits on your posters and flyers, you could even put a small laser print on every seat in the venue saying "written and directed by" but at this point you are trying to get people in through the door – another 6 words could have been saved.

Possible saving of 11 words = Eleven words which could have been used for a better description.

Cumbernauld Smith And Waxington Gorge – The Queen's Knickers

Cumbernauld Smith and Waxington Gorge present The Queen's Knickers – running time approximately 50 minutes. A colourful collection of carefully crafted comedy characters, skits and sketches. Prepare for 'pun-ishment'.

Again there's repetition of the company name, which doesn't look bad, it's just they could have saved words by dropping the surnames – saving 2 words. Repeating the show's title is a complete waste of words – saving 3 words. The running time of the show is in the details at the bottom of the listing; in any case how long it lasts isn't really a selling point – saving 5 words. Sketches and skits are the same thing – could have saved 2 more word.

Possible saving of 11 words = you start noticing ways to save words reading old Fringe guides.

Gonzalez And Graham

<u>Gonzalez and Graham</u> bring you <u>an hour of sketch comedy</u> the likes of which no man or woman has ever seen before. "Very funny" – Fife Gazette.

Again show name repeated in listing, as is information from the genre guide and the fact the show is listed in the comedy section. Possible saving of 7 words. Here are seven words they could have added there: "that press quote looks fishy to me".

BLURB HINTS AND TIPS

* Use the full name of the performer in show titles but in the blurb reduce it to just a first name or nickname. This is a good way to save a word. It also personalises the performer.

* Remember there is a genre guide for shows including stand-up, improv, musical, cabaret and burlesque. No point repeating these in the blurb.

COPYRIGHT OF 40 WORD BLURB

The forementioned real show descriptions from the 2010 and 2011 Fringe programme, and are reproduced with kind permission from the Edinburgh Fringe Festival Society who retain their copyright.

Upon listing the show with the Fringe office you hand over copyright of your show description to them. This legal technicality allows the Fringe office to freely distribute the description to as many different publications as they need to without each performer having to be contacted individually to gain their permission before the material can be distributed, usually to third party websites, newspapers and other publications.

ADVERT IN THE OFFICIAL FRINGE GUIDE

A quarter page advert in the Fringe guide will cost around £1000. This can make your show more noticeable to those quickly browsing through the guide.

FRINGE ADVERT HINTS AND TIPS

Shows can share an advert to cut down on cost. The Fringe office has no problem with this. Sharing an advert has the possible disadvantage of reducing the impact of the advert for each show. Conversely, a shared advert of two related shows can increase the profile of both. Consider the overall effect of shared marketing.

PR PEOPLE

The main job of a PR – public relations – person is to try to get you press coverage, make other contacts and arrange other events that will help market you and the show.

Quotations for PR people are varied. Prices start at £300 plus VAT and go up to as much as £1500 plus VAT. That's a lot of ticket sales to break even on that one. £1800 divided by £5.88 equals 306 ticket sales. However if the PR person is really good and worked their magic on someone in TV production and, as a result, you got an appearance on a panel show, then you might get your money back on the TV fee. For performers the Fringe is a way of selling yourself, not just the show and, since you're not going to be getting rich quick, long term profit and career prospects may well be your objective.

For those producing plays good press can lead to productions moving on to the West End or a regional theatre tour afterwards; where again the money could be recouped. The BBC pays more for adaptations of existing material to be turned into broadcast plays in the Afternoon or Saturday Play slot, than for material that has never been performed before. Critically well received productions are considerably easier to get commissioned than material that has never been performed. Broadcasters like the BBC receive numerous unsolicited manuscripts each week. It stands to reason that an unsolicited script from an unknown writer can quite easily end up in a pile with similar scripts, whereas a submission from a well received play at the Fringe looks much more professional and interesting.

Sketch shows can also benefit from the services of PR. Again decent press can also help the show move on the West End or a regional tour.

In 2010 I interviewed a number of known critics at the Fringe and on the subject of PR people they had varying opinions. Most of them conceded that PR people had persuaded them to go and see a show at some point but none had ever influenced a positive review being written. Steve Bennett[5] from Chortle.co.uk said, "say there's a choice between two sketch shows I've not heard of and one is PRed and the other isn't, I might be tempted to go with the first as it shows a certain belief in their own show that they've employed one".

You need to get recommendations before you hire someone. As with all tradespeople, everyone's happy to charge you but quality can vary greatly. In 2004, Chris Smith received a full refund from his PR person after they acknowledged that they hadn't done anywhere near the work they should have to promote his show. While the refund didn't leave him out of pocket he had missed the opportunity that effective PR might have bought him at the Fringe. He would have to wait a year to try again and there's no way to compensate for lost time and opportunity.

You may also want to check up on what your PR people are doing. I spoke with one act whose PR had promised to

---

[5] Full interview available at http://theianfox.wordpress.com

get a reviewer in from The Scotsman; one of the more highly respected publications that reviews shows at the Fringe. The act said that if the PR person could not bring a reviewer he could arrange it himself, as he knew someone at The Scotsman who had offered help. The PR person insisted that wouldn't be necessary as everything was in hand, so the act left it to her. Someone did indeed come from The Scotsman. They watched the show and a few others at the venue but no reviews were published. When the act rang The Scotsman to find out why these reviews had never seen the light of day despite having been told by his PR person that they were withheld due to lack of space, it turned out that the individual who'd been was a staff member at the paper, but not as a reviewer. They'd just come along for the free ticket. As a result, the opportunity for a real review from a real critic was lost.

PRESS RELEASE

If you have a PR company, the press release is their responsibility. If you are doing your own PR you need to put together a release around May so it's ready to be sent out when the Fringe guide is published in June.

A press release needs to be useful to a variety of audiences. Publications may want to do a write-up of your show, reviewers might want to get an idea of what your show is about before they attend. Others might use it to decide whether they think your show is worthy of their interest at all.

If someone has taken an interest in your show, your press release should be a useful source of information so they can get facts right.

Once you have produced a concise and interesting press release then send a copy to the Fringe office so as they can also circulate it, your venue's press office – if they have one and to anyone who might read it. You should also put it somewhere on the internet where it can be easily downloaded.

There are no set rules for what should go in your press release but here are some ideas:

* Full names of the performers.

* Background information about you and the show.

* Reviews from previous years.

* Quotes from people involved in putting the show together.

* Unusual facts related to the show.

* Human interest stories surrounding the show.

* Memorable claims to fame for you or the show.

If you get your press release right, it can make the journalists and reviewers pay attention; and a well-written press release sent at the right time can create other opportunities too. Ashley Frieze's press release for 'The Seven Deadly Sings' in 2010 caught the attention of an editor for a Sunday newspaper who later commissioned him to write a feature on the content of the show; the fee for which pretty much paid for his Fringe production costs.

When writing a release consider how pushed for time – and lazy – some journalists are. They haven't the time – or simply can't be bothered – to read through a huge volumes. Ideally they would like a ready-made package they can work with.

Some tips for how to make your press release journalist friendly:

* Don't overly format the text – as they'll have to undo it if

they copy and paste it.

* Provide the text of the press release both in the body of your email and as an attachment in a useful document format – Microsoft Word is possibly best.

* Try to write the majority of the information in 200 words as though it was a write-up of the show.

* Provide extended information later but at the top make everything short and snappy to give them a quick picture of the show.

* Provide links to good quality images they can use for publication.

* Include the words PRESS RELEASE in big letters right at the top.

If in doubt look for other shows' press releases and see what grabs your attention in theirs.

POSTERS IN VENUES AND ADDITIONAL LOCATIONS

Local distribution companies will put posters up around the city in cafés, pubs, betting shops and anywhere that will allow them to. The advantage of these companies is that you don't have to wander around with Blu Tack and a bag of paper restricted by your own knowledge of Edinburgh and how bold you're feeling about asking permission to put up the posters. The disadvantage is that the postering companies do not necessarily put your posters in places where your audience might be found.

Distribution companies have a bigger sway in where they are allowed to put posters up, enabling them to get more posters for more shows up around the city. Smaller shows generally manage quite well without using poster distribution but you need to get in there quickly before they take up all the good wall space.

If you do not arrive in Edinburgh very long before your first performance you may be advised to get someone to put your posters up so there is some coverage of your existence before you look at your first day's box office figures.

A3 or A4 posters distributed around the city in bars, clubs, takeaways, cafés costs approximately £210. Divided by £5.88 you have to sell 35 tickets to recover your costs.

Most companies won't distribute any less than 300 posters.

Lamp Post Wraps – three sided plastic structures placed around lamp posts, poles, road signs and trees – are approved by the council and all sites are official. 10 posters around the Fringe area will cost around £60 – inclusive of VAT. Divided by £5.88 you have to sell 10 tickets to the cost back. Again this doesn't include the cost of the poster.

Triangle Posters Large posters approximately one metre by 2 metres. These can cost up to £1000 for the 4 weeks of the festival. Divided by £5.88 that's 170 tickets. Again price doesn't include cost of the poster.

FLYERS

Flyers are best handed out on a one to one basis. Static flyering, which is leaving piles of paper in and around venues, doesn't work and is a waste of paper. The fine art of flyering is a specialist technique and has its own section later on.

Prices for 5000 range from £50 to £120 and VAT is not applicable.

ADDITIONAL ADVERTISING

Be wary of a lot of the people contacting you about additional advertising. Firstly if the person is using the Press Contact List published by the Fringe office to ring you, they're not that reputable. The Press List is for press interviews, not selling advertising.

In 2010 a friend of mine bought an advert on a Fringe related website for £50. He was told it would be on a rotation basis with about 4 other adverts. I had to reload the web page 12 times before his advert showed up. I doubt that advert sold £50 worth of tickets for him.

Based on the above figures and how much you receive from ticket sales. I would work out how many tickets the advert has to sell for you to get your money back from it. Let's say an advert in another publication costs £50 plus VAT. £60 divided by £5.88 it has to sell you approximately 10 tickets.

Be wise to opportunities to get your advert out for free. Read the promotions that come through from the Fringe. Some places will put a banner ad up for free in exchange for a bit of content for their website or smart phone app. Overall, if you want to get an audience then put a decent image and 40 words in the Fringe guide and be prepared to go out there and charm people into your show.

Advertising and flyering are the conventional methods of spreading the word and they work, up to a point. Ultimately, everyone is doing it and so the audience eventually becomes poster blind, flyer phobic and generally disinterested. Unconventional and original methods of advertising really catch people's attention. Out of the box thinking can serve you well.

THINKING OUTSIDE THE BOX

By far the most effective means of promoting anything. Do something someone else isn't doing and you'll get more attention than them. This is where going to the festival before you go up there to do your first show is helpful because it gives you an idea of what the place looks and feels like and it is much easier to have ideas about something when you have an image of it in your mind.

Case Study: Tim Vine

In 2006 on Cowgate right in the heart of the Fringe area on the site of the former Gilded Balloon, a 60 feet wide by 10 feet high billboard appeared. The photo was of Tim wearing a black suit with a red shirt holding his arms out. The background was his name in lights, and it simply read "TIM VINE is not appearing at this year's Edinburgh Festival."

People walking past laughed at it and it even picked up 5 star reviews. Questions were asked: How much had that cost? What was the point?

It's hard to say exactly what this achieved, except perhaps a presence at the Fringe and continued repeat business for Tim's show the following year. It was probably a cheaper way to make those people who saw it laugh than to run a show and make a loss. In any case I'm sure it didn't harm DVD sales at all.

Case Study: Lewis Schaffer

In 2005 the Edinburgh Comedy Award dropped its sponsorship deal with Perrier after twenty four years. The following year Intelligent Finance – a division of HBOS – took over sponsorship in a three year deal. After the banking crisis in 2009 the deal wasn't renewed and it looked like the awards were going to be without a sponsor. Then a press release marked as being from the awards boss "Nika Burns" started circulating announcing that the awards had managed to find a sponsor – American comic Lewis Schaffer was taking over. In a deal worth £99 per year, the awards were now going to be known as 'The Lewies' in his honour.

It wasn't long before the real Nica Burns – the correct spelling – issued a response through her solicitor threatening legal action against Lewis citing "whilst our client would not be involved with a significant comedy award if she was bereft of a sense of humour, this has gone too far." The press release was exposed as a spoof but according to the BBC website The List magazine had been persuaded it was real.

The net result of coverage in various broadsheets lead to Lewis getting the 2009 Malcolm Hardee Cunning Stunt Award.

Case Study: Kunt And The Gang

In 2011 Kunt and the Gang and Bob Slayer shared the Malcolm Hardee Cunning Stunt Award after an interesting three weeks of a publicity stunt dubbed "Cockgate". At the beginning of the festival Kunt handed out stickers with a cartoon cock on them to his audience on their way out of his show. Audience members starting adding them to other shows' posters in an amusing way. Anyone with an open mouth was an obvious target, as well as other posters where the person in the image was bending over or holding something in their hand[6]. What started as a prank – Kunt most likely defaced his fair share of text books when he

---

[6] I photographed a number of defaced posters and put together a gallery of them on my blog site http://theianfox.wordpress.com or Google "Ian Fox Cockgate"

was at school – all of a sudden became the one thing everyone was talking about. The bigger venues complained to Edinburgh City Council asking for stickers to be removed from their posters and a council worker gave Kunt a strict talking to explaining that he'd had to spend the day "pulling off over a hundred cocks". The Scottish press and Fringe media picked it up, the story was funny, and it spun out of control for the next three weeks – even though it had been over and done with in the first few days.

Good ideas go viral and being memorable can make as much of a difference to your audience numbers as having an amazing show.

HOW TO KNOW IF WHAT YOU'VE DONE HAS WORKED

If someone is threatening you with legal action the chances are you've probably got the publicity you were after.

SO HOW DO YOU MAKE MONEY?

Firstly you have try and save money wherever possible. Some shows miss the advert in the Fringe guide. Some venues might insist on an advert, but they won't know if you've actually got an advert until the Fringe guide comes out by which point it will be too late for them to say anything about it. That might well be a good saving of a thousand pounds. £1000 buys you a lot of flyering time.

The new format in the Fringe guide with an image for every show has possibly damaged the effectiveness of adverts. I know of three shows with adverts in the 2010 Fringe guide that struggled with audience numbers. One show was cancelled after the first week as only 1 out of 7 shows went ahead. The other two struggled for numbers throughout the Fringe and had to pull some performances.

A third option is to rent a cheaper venue. Some venues don't have the same prestige as others – let's be clear about that up front. If you're there to get seen by TV people you need to be in one of the venues they're likely to be found hanging around: Pleasance, Assembly, Gilded Balloon and Underbelly. However if you successfully create a buzz around yourself you can easily tempt industry types into some of the cheaper venues. In 2010, Imran Yusuf – performing a free show –had the BBC's 'Culture Show' reporting on him such was his success and buzz surrounding him. I know this because the 'Picnic' was on the next floor and ran about the same time. Thanks to Imran, I got to give the BBC's presenter Kirsty 'the thinking man's crumpet' Wark directions out of the building after she had watched his show.

FIND YOUR OWN PEOPLE

A lot of the production companies employ flyering teams and pay them by the hour. They then invoice the client for each hour they flyer. Usually there will be a difference in what the client pays per hour and what the flyering staff receive. One way to avoid paying mark-ups is to find your own staff and employ them directly. Tap into the right groups on Facebook and you can find flyering staff directly. Try searching for the Flyerer Network.

Paid venues don't supply a technician to run the lights and sound in your show for free. There will be a fee at a set rate per performance. Usually you can find your own technician to work cheaper than the venue's rates. You might well be able to save money on a tech by only using them for the first few minutes of the show. As sound desks are usually located at the back of the room they can usually slip out without the audience noticing once the show has started. Be aware that the set up at the paid venues can be rather complex so you need to hire someone competent, rather than rope in a clueless mate.

DO YOUR OWN PR

If you work out what press you want you can try to target them yourself. Look at the publications you want to get coverage from and use some detective work to get the contact details for the people you want to contact. The Fringe office produces a fairly impressive press list and it's worth using it.

One word of advice, if you are going to do this have a good show. If you're new and not fully formed as a performer don't waste their time. You only get one chance to make a good first impression. Drag them along to a poor show and it might be years before you can get them back again. Be honest with yourself, have you put enough work into the show?

DON'T PAY FOR A VENUE

Another option is to not pay for a venue at all. The free venues are becoming increasingly attractive to performers and producers. They're not ideal but then neither is paying over £4000 and finding yourself in a Portakabin for three weeks. Free shows, with generous audiences filling a collection bucket can be surprisingly lucrative.

DOES ANYONE MAKE MONEY ON THEIR SHOW?

The production companies make it very difficult for you to make money for yourself. Unfortunately due to libel laws and the fact that I've been told things privately in conversation I can't publish performer names without their permission, and as the contents of business information is subject to copyright laws I'm going to have to use vague descriptions and pseudonyms to illustrate this example.

CASE STUDY: COMIC A

Comic A was recently on a stadium tour of the UK and is a

well-known face on TV. Before they became a household name, in fact just before it happened, their show in a small room sold out completely. An additional show was also added in a larger venue in the final weekend of the festival. Total takings for their show came in at £21,000. Upon presentation of the final figures it was revealed that the venue and production company managed to rack up £19,500 in expenses and commissions. Comic A was left with about £1500 which they'd have to pay tax on; based on 25 performances this meant that they had received around £50 per gig.

Unbelievably, a lot of this money had been spent advertising shows that were already sold out. This is common practice with some companies. What they're actually trying to do is demonstrate how successful they and the performer are, by highlighting that their shows are sold out.

CASE STUDY: ASHLEY FRIEZE AND THE COSTS OF A FREE SHOW

I performed my solo show – the Seven Deadly Sings – in both 2010 and 2011. It was a musical stand-up show and required me to use a lot of musical instruments, which I recall buying at some point. To give you an idea of what it's like to run a free show at the Fringe I've pulled these figures from my accounts as a fair representation of my core costs and revenues. I'd expect them to apply to an average solo show.

REGISTRATION FEES

The Fringe registration costs £295, more if you register a bit later. My show was with the Free Festival, which asks for £40 towards admin and printing costs for the Free Festival programme.

For my show to exist, I had to pay £335.

EQUIPMENT

For any Fringe show you should travel light, but you may still have some props. I spent £63. I bought books to read quotes from and CDs with music I used in the show. I also had a vinyl banner printed with graphics on it large enough to be seen from the back of the room. Spending a little on getting quality props can make your show seem more professional and enables your props to survive being set-up and put away 20 or so times.

PUBLICITY MATERIALS

I purchased 50 posters, which cost about £25 from www.fileprint.org and 5000 flyers, which cost £50 or so from www.1-2-print.co.uk. Without these important publicity tools your show can easily go unnoticed.

PRODUCTION STAFF

The worst thing about producing a solo show yourself is that you have minimal help. With free venues there are no technical or front of house staff helping you, so it can be even more isolating. I chose to find someone to help me manage the room during the show and help with the set-up and tear down of each performance. I paid them £150 for the whole run, which was 16 shows. There are a lot of students in Edinburgh over the Fringe capable, willing and interested in the Fringe experience.

Without the help of my techie, I would have been a nervous wreck before we even hit the first minute of performance. It was money well spent.

PREVIEWS

It's essential to try out your material before you hit Edinburgh and I set up a preview at a Fringe venue in

London in the June before my Edinburgh run. I had to hire this venue at £140 for the night and had to produce posters for the show, costing me £7. A lot of friends and well-wishers attended giving me £135 in ticket sales, so my own preview cost me £13 to stage.

I also did a number of paid preview performances before Edinburgh. These were paid at £20 here, £50 there, etc. I managed, across four particularly good previews, to raise £170 towards the costs of my show and hone the material at the same time.

SOMEWHERE TO LIVE

Edinburgh flats can be expensive, but they are an important base of operations and a calm place to go between the madness of the Fringe. I paid £650 for the rent of a double room for 2 weeks in a shared 3 bedroom flat. This is a reasonable rate. People will pay a lot more for less.

REVENUE

The collection bucket at my show for 16 days, in a 50 seater venue, on average managed to get me about £2 per audience member. I had collections that were something like:

£40, £75, £50, £70, £25, £60, £70, £40, £35, £35, £50, £50, £40, £40, £80, £75

Weekends were good, Saturdays especially. Some days were just quiet. My energy and voice wore out about two thirds of the way in and I had a couple of unappreciated days. Things picked up for the final weekend. Total collection bucket – £835

TOTAL COSTS

In setting up the show, paying for my preview, buying publicity, renting and paying my techie, I spent £1420.

The revenues from the previews I performed, along with the door money, raised me £1140.

Therefore my Fringe experience cost me £280.

BOTTOM LINE

I lost the equivalent of the Fringe registration fee. I think that's a fair price for a Fringe show.

For £140 a week – £20 a day – I had two weeks of refining my act and enjoying myself in Edinburgh. That's cheaper than you'd pay for a camping trip.

This is peanuts compared to how much it's possible to lose in a single day at a larger paid venue. I can earn £280 by performing two well-paid stand-up gigs at comedy clubs.

WHAT DID THE MONEY BUY ME?

I was able to perform a show that was well received, which got better over the course of the Fringe. I had a great time. I had some people tell me that they'd enjoyed my show and had seen it multiple times. I got some YouTube clips of my show in action and some online followers. I networked with other acts and performed with them at other gigs in the following year.

Overall I had a good time without losing my shirt.

PRE FRINGE PROMOTION

GET THE NAME OF YOUR SHOW RIGHT

I don't wish to single out people here for making bad choices but the name of your show is important. In some cases it's going to be potential audience members only piece of information about your show. The listings board outside venues are a major way of getting people into both free and paid shows. There isn't room on them to include the 40 words describing what a show is about. Your show title needs to be as punchy and informative as possible. The title needs to get across an idea of the show in about six words.

Good examples of titles include 'Shaggers' – comedians doing shagging material, 'The Jocks and Geordies' – comics from Scotland and Newcastle, 'Pick of the Fringe', 'Comedy Countdown', 'Late'N'Live'. A snappy title really helps you sell your show.

Since 2010 I've designed the Free Festival booklet. The biggest problem I have is fitting everything into 8 pages. When you lose a page for the front cover, the introduction on the inside page, adverts and a map of the venues, there are only four and a bit pages left to get every show listing into. When in excess of 60,000 copies of the Free Festival booklet are being printed, adding another page to the booklet would increase the printing cost dramatically. The only fair way to do it is for each show to get exactly the same size space, consequently the only way to fit 'Don't Be a Comedian in Northern Ireland While Drinking Your Buckfast Under a Bridge' into a box the same size as everyone else's was to shrink the lettering to a size just above a microdot making it really hard to read. I don't think that helped sell the show, calling the show 'Irishfellas' might have been more helpful.

LIST IN THE FRINGE GUIDE – FREE SHOW SPECIFIC ADVICE

You're obliged to list the show in the Fringe guide if you do a Free Festival show but not if you do a PBH Free Fringe show. Listing your show makes it look legitimate and it makes you an official part of the Fringe with box office support, performer services, discounts and other benefits. Although I usually produce Free shows, I allocate tickets when I list the show with the Fringe office. This might seem odd as they are free shows but it's an extra way of advertising your show that doesn't cost anything so it's worth doing. For audiences who plan their day, it gives them another ticket to hold and allows them to feel they've committed to your show. Audiences members that turn up with tickets have definitely decided to see your show and have an idea of why they are there, making for a better atmosphere.

PICNIC TICKETS

Having tickets for the 'Picnic' only came about by accident in 2008, after I had a rather strange phone call from the Fringe office in April. In the show's blurb for that year I'd included the line "free tickets, free Tibet!" The person from the Fringe office wanted me to edit the listing, at first I assumed it was the free Tibet line that they wanted rid of, but their objection was I couldn't say "free tickets" as there were no tickets for the show. I can't remember what they wanted me to change the listing to, but I do remember I wasn't impressed with their suggestion. The Fringe office then suggested this compromise of issuing tickets for the show, which I went along with and then completely forgot about. In August we started doing the show and noticed that around twenty percent of our audience were arriving with tickets for the show. I've allocated tickets with the Fringe office ever since.

MARKETING MATERIALS

POSTERS

Posters need to be eye catching and if it's comedy in my opinion they should be funny in some way, sexy can also work. I have a better chance at the first one than the second. In venues posters are displayed in very close proximity to each other so they need to stand out. If you are doing a free show you shouldn't need any more than 100 posters or to put them up anywhere other than free venues. Fly posting incurs a £75 fine and sticking posters up on the approved poster stands on the Royal Mile is nothing more than a waste of paper – two minutes later someone will paste over them.

Paid venues will ask for specific quantities of posters and will put them up in the venue for you. Distribution companies will agree to post a certain number of posters for you. It's a good idea to have spare posters so you can make some repairs to important poster sites during the Fringe, but you probably only need to keep 5 – 10% of your posters in reserve for this.

For free shows I think that A3 is the best size as there is limited space inside the venues to display them. They also get torn down quite often in venues that are nightclubs in the evening and have to be replaced. Bigger posters are more expensive and so your replacement costs are higher. Portrait format makes your life easier when it comes to putting them up.

Paid venues will have specifications for what size they want them to be. Usually they stipulate portrait format and require logos and other text printed on them.

POSTER CONCEPTS

I really enjoy working out ideas for poster concepts. You need to be creative with your imagery. Every year I've seen at least one company do a pastiche of the 'Trainspotting' or 'Being John Malkovich' posters: they are clichés at the Fringe and have been done to death.

Furthermore, try to avoid doing a pastiche of the big hit movies of the year. It's way too easy to come up with the same idea as someone else if you're picking up on a big cultural icon. The same could be said for spoofs of major works of art too. I came up with a poster concept one year based on a Magritte's 'Son of Man' painting – self-portrait with an apple in front of his face. When the Fringe guide was published in June I discovered an advert recreating the same painting. At that point I needed a rethink.

I usually design the posters for 'The Great Big Comedy Picnic' in July once the Fringe guide has come out. That way I can avoid producing something similar to what someone else is using. This doesn't always work unfortunately. The poster for my show 'Ian Fox Exposes Himself' was a mock-up of a front page tabloid newspaper, the same year Steve N Allen did his topical comedy show 'Some News,' the poster for which looked like a tabloid front page. I had to make sure I my positioned my posters far enough away from Steve's so there was no confusion between the two shows.

Consider the poster image – what else can it be used for? Does it work on a T-Shirt? Does it look good on your flyers as well as the poster? Will it look good on the web? It's worth pointing out that web images are usually landscape, so you'll have to adapt portrait format posters for the internet. Having a consistent image that looks good on all media, can really help reinforce your message.

For the 'Picnic' we often come up with a tag line for the

show and then build an image around it. One year we were "Homemade heroes of comedy" and so used photos of the cast in makeshift superhero outfits. Another year we were "Flirting with bankruptcy" so had photos of ourselves in white vests either eating baked beans out of tin or slugging whisky straight out of the bottle. Think of how you're describing your show and have some fun with it.

If you hand out flyers yourself, then your image will be something you can use as a talking point with the people you give them to, so bear that in mind when you're designing the posters. Also bear in mind that you will find at least one of your flyers in a gutter at some point.

GET A DESIGNER

It's best if someone who knows what they're doing designs them for you. You're paying for a large number of reproductions – a minimum of 5000 flyers and 50 posters. This work needs to be done by someone who knows the difference between a 72dpi and 300dpi image, what CMYK colours are, what converting letters to shapes and rasterisation in Adobe Photoshop means. What the correct amount of bleed to use around the edge of a print is and what file formats printers prefer you to send in. If your show is good, but your poster looks like you did it in the library using Microsoft Word, it can put an audience off.

The sad fact is that there are hundreds of shows out there with professional designers making brilliant posters for them. Their show may be nothing compared to yours, but the audience can't tell that from the poster alone. The bar is set high.

WHAT INFORMATION TO INCLUDE

* Title of the show and artist name. Best to include both in my opinion, some people think that including your name in big letters is nothing more than an ego trip, but in

conversation people will just ask for "Ian Fox's show", and it makes it easier for venue staff that don't know you to point people in the right direction for your show.

* The dates and times of the show. This may seem obvious but unfortunately I have seen shows print 5000 flyers with no mention of what time the show was on.

* A brief description of the show – optional. Ideally the title of the show should really indicate what the show is about. Adding a strap line may be more eye catching than a couple of paragraphs of your world views.

* Press reviews – optional. Star ratings look good, but only from well-known publications. Go for something short and snappy. Editing a bad review to try and make it look like a good review usually looks pretty obvious.

* Venue, artist management and production company logos. It's often a contractual requirement to include the venue's logo anyway; however from a design point of view I find that they tend to make the poster look more like a show poster.

* Posters for comedy shows work better when they're designed by people who know about comedy. Designers can produce artwork that looks aesthetically pleasing but they don't always give it the right feel for comedy shows. A designer who did the programmes for the Manchester Comedy Festival one year had the idea of ironically using sad faces to advertise the festival. The finished posters looked more like an NHS mental health campaign rather than a comedy festival.

POSTER HINTS AND TIPS

PHOTOSHOP LICENCE

If you're familiar with how to operate Adobe Photoshop or a similar package but you can't afford to purchase the licence you can usually do all the work you need in the 30 day trial period. Alternatively there is a similar open source programme called Gimp, which is rich on features but relatively low on usability. Cloud computing sites are fairly limited when it comes to designing posters as they can't output files in the correct formats for printers.

THE BLACK BAR

Placing a black bar at the bottom of the poster for the details of the show and relevant logos is not only the most efficient way of relaying the information to audience members but it can also save you time and money. If the details of the performance are not integral to the body of the image, the poster image is easily reusable without any redesign costs. For example, if you're previewing the show you can simply send the image file to the promoter and they can print out the details on a white piece of paper and then staple it over the details of the Edinburgh show.

It's a common sight on the last night of the Fringe to see performers taking down posters from the venue that are still reasonably clean. The initial assumption is that they're simply taking some souvenirs but they're not. They're recycling: they send the posters to somewhere they're performing the show again and the venue prints out and attaches the new details. That black bar at the bottom of the poster can save the environment and cut your printing costs in one 4cm high fell swoop.

Fileprint.org is a handy site for getting a small run of poster prints. They'll print high quality colour prints from PDF files for about 50p each. This is not quite as good as full colour lithographic poster printing and is closer to a very high quality print from a desktop printer, but in the low level lighting conditions of most venues it's difficult to tell the difference.

PROOF READING PRINT OUTS

Most design programmes have a spell check built into them but you still need to print out a copy on your home printer and get as many people as possible to check it for glaring errors. You also need to give those people a copy of your show details so they can check the information you've put down is accurate, not just spelt correctly. I managed to print the wrong time and dates on my posters in 2005.

COLOUR PROOFS

Printers quite often charge to send you a proof copy of your artwork. A quick and easy way of seeing what your work looks like printed, to make sure colours are correct and that nothing is pixelated[7] is to output the poster file as a JPG and then take it to a photo printing machine and have it printed. This service usually costs about 30p per print and is available in many high street shops and supermarkets.

TECHNICAL SPECIFICATIONS

CMYK colour. Computer monitors display colours as RGB which allows for millions of colours on a computer screen. Printers only have so many colours they can print out. These colours are based on mixing cyan, yellow and magenta inks. Convert the image to CMYK as soon as possible and check to see if your printer has any template

---

[7] A blocky or blurry image caused by not having a high enough resolution file or enough megapixels on your camera.

files for Photoshop that have the correct colour profiles already set up.

Bleed. To produce an A6 flyer, printers don't print on a piece of paper that is exactly A6 in size; they print on a larger piece of paper and then cut the paper down to the right size. When you prepare artwork you have to add an extra 3mm to the canvas size making the document bigger than it needs to be. This term is called bleed. You shouldn't include any text within 5mm of the edge. You should however continue your background image to avoid having a white edge on the finished flyer. The printer will use a guillotine to cut the flyer down to the correct size, if the paper moves slightly during the cutting process the flyers will still be serviceable.

Convert lettering to shapes. Commercial printing companies have few fonts installed on their machines so you need to convert lettering in your file to a shape or rasterize it in Adobe Photoshop, so as the file is portable and will output correctly from any computer. This way you don't need to send any fonts to the printer and the printed out edges of your lettering will be smooth not zigzagged. Tiny mistakes like this affect the overall image quality of the artwork and make it look unprofessional.

Flatten image. Final stage of file preparation is to flatten all layers to make the file as small as possible.

PDF output. Most printers request PDF files. These should be exported as press quality, deselect the 'preserve photoshop editing capability' option to reduce file size. Printers also ask for multiple page PDF files, effectively both sides of your flyer in one file. That way they don't mix up the files from different clients. Consult the help files in your programme to find out how to produce a multiple page PDF file.

NOT AS PROFICIENT AS THEY THOUGHT

In 2006 one comedy agent decided to produce all the posters in house for the show they were promoting. Evidently they were not as proficient with Photoshop as they thought they were. The following year their printers produced a guide detailing what not to do when designing posters. Nearly every example included was this agent's efforts.

PRINT ORDERS

If you are the only person flyering for your show you should only need to order 5000 flyers. 5000 is the standard unit for ordering flyers in – if you try and order less it ends up costing you more as the printers have to reset their machinery. Based on 24 shows, an order of 5000 means you'll be handing out 208 per day. If you're targeting your potential punters and actually engaging them in conversation and not blindly passing out bits of paper then this should be about right, with some left for the recycle centre and a handful of souvenirs. If you are employing a flyering team then it will depend on how many hours a day you are employing them for. Calculate your order based on them giving out 200 every three hours – approximately one per minute.

As mentioned already 100 posters is more than enough for free shows.

FLYERS

The front side of a flyer is usually the poster image. For the reverse side of the flyer you have a few different options:

1) Blurb about the show, different photos and a map showing where the venue is.

2) Repeat the image from the front.

3) Something else entirely.

4) The poster image for another show. Effectively a way to cut the cost of your flyers in half – share a flyer with another show.

No one ever knows what to put on the back of a flyer. Most go for a map to the venue and some more information about the show. It's a good idea and makes it easier to tell people where the show is. My favourite flyer of the 2010 Fringe didn't do that. Kunt and the Gang created a handy "have you shit yourself guide?" a series of yes and no questions in boxes with arrows getting you to the correct answer. Not only did this fit in with the tone of the show, it was funny. It sold the show better than any press quotes or mentioning non-winning positions in comedy competitions.

For reasons unknown, when most people are handed a flyer they immediately turn it over[8]. This is a possible disadvantage of sharing flyer space with another show and illustrates why the back needs as much attention as the front.

* Avoid using cheap printers that only produce one sided flyers. Double sided flyers aren't more expensive if you use the right printer. http://www.1-2-print.co.uk/ charge approximately £45 for 5000 including delivery.

PROMOTIONAL ITEMS

I've never managed to get around to doing this yet. You can get good deals on T-shirts and hoodies, printed with your show details on. To get the best deals you need to

---

[8] I have to say I particularly noticed this in 2013. I put an advert for this book on the back of my show flyers. Straight away punters would turn the flyer around look at the book ad instead of the show poster and then just look confused.

order them well in advance of the festival as some online printers can take up to three weeks to deliver. They make a nice souvenir once the festival is over. As for whether these items help you get punters is anyone's guess. With the climate in Scotland I'd recommend having something waterproof made. If you're ordering T-shirts to wear whilst out flyering, remember that they will need washing. Wash one shirt every day for 25 days and it's not going to look as good at the end of the festival as it did at the beginning.

WHAT TO DO ONCE THE FESTIVAL STARTS

Aside from getting to Edinburgh in time to start your show, you need to be at your venue the day before your first performance for the 'get in' – where you bring in any major props or equipment and have a technical rehearsal enabling your show staff to work out lighting and music cues. These are usually scheduled by the venue.

You also need to find time, when you're not attending launch parties and schmoozing journalists, to read through your script and commit as much of it to memory as possible.

If you're performing in a free show you also need to wander all over Edinburgh putting up your posters in the other free venues to try and attract a crowd. If you're in a paid show don't bother wandering all around the free venues putting up posters for your show. If you're not performing in a free venue, the posters will be removed. Moreover, it's unlikely that a PBH Free Fringe poster will stay up for long in a Laughing Horse Free Festival venue and vice versa.

Whether you're in a paid or free venue, you need to hit the streets with some flyers.

If you are new to Edinburgh take a walk around, find your kind of cafés and supermarkets and maybe work out some useful short cuts between places – especially if they take you past reliable toilets. Many venues have abysmal toilet facilities – if in doubt go for university buildings, coffee chains or high price hotels. I often wander into hotel receptions "looking for someone I'm supposed to meet," or enquiring "does the bar do take away coffee?"

PLANNING TO DO STUFF WHILE YOU'RE THERE

Making plans of things to do whilst you're in Edinburgh and the festival is going on around you is a difficult one. The problem is going home and writing a 300 word blog piece about your day or recording a podcast for your website is extremely difficult when all you want to do is crawl under a duvet and sleep. It's also probably something you shouldn't be trying to do when that quick drink after your show turned into several slow ones and all of a sudden it was 3am and the bar was closing.

The Fringe is a full on assault on the senses. All the colours, the noise and the costumes leave you mentally tired. Combine that with walking the streets of Edinburgh, which is possibly more physical exercise in a day than you are used to, and exhaustion becomes your number one enemy. There are only so many hours in the day. Before your show you have to concentrate on drumming up a crowd. Post show you'll want to relax or you might have another show to go and perform in.

Extra shows are good as they give you something to do, and having something else to do once you've finished is helpful, but it's hard work if you have go out and do the same thing over and over again. Ideally if you're doing a second show, then what you want to do is find one where you can just turn up and perform without any of the pressures of running it.

In 2005 I was in Seymour Mace's show 'Imaginary Friends Reunited'. Show time was around 9pm, my show finished at around 6pm. I only had a couple of small parts in Seymour's show and a three hour break between the two shows meant plenty of time to eat dinner and have a rest. Christian Knowles Productions were producing Seymour's show so they did all the marketing and flyering, Seymour did the bulk of the work, all I had to do was turn up. I even got a night off half way through the run. This was an ideal second show to be in.

In 2009 Gill Smith produced a show called 'News at Tenish,' a topical comedy show made up of 3 or 4 comics each night. For this I just had to turn up and do some jokes about stuff that was in the paper that day. I didn't even have to do all of the shows. These are the kind of gigs you want to get: stage time and opportunity to try out new ideas and jokes and no responsibility whatsoever for getting a crowd in.

MANAGING YOUR SHOW

You need to be in your show space 25 minutes before you start, assuming the handover time between shows is 15 minutes. This doesn't include any time you need to get into costume or arrange props if you're doing a more theatrical show.

In free venues you need to check that the sound system is working, move any furniture around, adjust any lighting and do any technical set-up you need to do. In a paid venue there may be staff there to help you, but you should aim to be ahead of the game rather than allowing the performance to suffer from avoidable problems as you set up. Moreover, if you arrive for the last ten minutes of the previous show you can take advantage of the situation if they finish early and can be set up before the audience are due in.

AUDIENCE SEATING PATTERNS

Shows work better when the audience are all sitting in the same place. The Fringe has unallocated seating and most audience members don't think about what's best for the show when they choose their seats. In a half empty room – common for most shows, the audience will often position themselves as far apart from each other as they can. Using someone to act as an usher to get them in the same place is the best way of getting them all where you want them: in the middle at the front. You can also close off one section of seats using a line of masking tape – removing the tape once the section is full – if you don't like ushering.

In paid venues you will have front of house staff helping, which generally avoids 'diluted audience syndrome.' In short, ushering works. Left to their own devices, audience members will sit in the wrong place, leap over masking tape and probably even hide near a power socket so they can cheekily charge their iPhone – it's happened more than once in shows I've been doing. If you can find someone to usher for you – or do it yourself – it will help. You can't always guarantee that the temporary staff in venues are aware that moving the audience around is part of their job. You need to keep an eye on the venue staff to see that they are doing what they are supposed to.

* If you're in a sketch show use one of the characters to do the ushering. It makes for a nice bit of audience interaction before the show starts.

MAKE FRIENDS WITH THE OTHER SHOWS

If you're doing twenty five shows in a row you'll be seeing the people in the slots before and after you every day. So it makes sense to be friendly with them. Help them tidy up after their show, ask them how it went, tell them the latest gossip. In 2010 the people in the incoming show told me about an incident the night before where a comedian had head-butted a heckler after a show – an interesting conversation. In 2011 I regularly chatted to the performer who followed my show, the actor George Innes. It was only after the first week I realised I recognised George from his earlier film work and got to chat to him about the making of 'The Italian Job' and 'Quadrophenia'.

Meeting other performers is an important part of the Fringe experience and it's well worth doing.

On the flip-side, if you don't have a good relationship with the other performers in the venue, things can go wrong. Tempers are more likely to get frayed if you accidentally overrun or something else goes wrong in the venue.

KIDS

We don't let them into 'The Great Big Comedy Picnic.' In the Fringe guide we list the show as 18+ and quietly tell anyone trying to bring their kids into the show that "sorry it's a licensed premise, no one under 18 is allowed," as a more diplomatic way of dealing with the situation. We find this makes things more comfortable for everyone. Ticketed venues can put restrictions on tickets marking them "over 18s only" and "contains strong language and material some people might find offensive."

Audience members can become uncomfortable if there is swearing and subject matter they don't consider suitable for children. The parents might be all right with it and the children are seldom personally offended, but the people around the family are the ones that you need to look out for. If you allow younger people into the show, you may need to make it safe for everyone.

From a punter's point of view Chris Judge told me, "*I saw Sean Collins in Edinburgh when there was a kid in the audience with his parents. Sean addressed it at the start of the show and interacted with them. He asked about the situation, told them there would be bad language, material some people would consider unsuitable for children and the parents and child said they were fine about it. Sean spent five minutes covering every angle that he could to make sure neither the parents, the child or the punters were remotely uncomfortable by the idea of any of it.*

I still felt uncomfortable when the adult material was being delivered and judging by the hesitant laughter from the rest of the room, I got the feeling I wasn't the only one."

Again you need to make sure the people doing your front of house management are aware that you don't want children in the show space if you decide to adopt this policy. Starting a show only to discover a family with children in the front row is uncomfortable as you have to try and mentally edit your show as you go along. It detracts from the performance.

Shows that are family friendly can often make more money in ticket sales, or, if they're a free show, in their collections. It's worth thinking about making your show family friendly since a lot of potential audience members are with their family and have a lot of time to fill. Free shows can be attractive to bigger groups, since a paid ticket, multiplied by the number of people in a family, is often an expensive hour for them. However, don't mis-market your show. If it's not family friendly, then keep the kids out.

NON-ENGLISH SPEAKING AUDIENCES

The Fringe is the world's largest arts festival. The population of the old town area of Edinburgh rises considerably during the festival with visitors from all over the world. Not all of them speak English and not all of them understand local references. You may have to tailor your material to an international audience. You have to recognise if you have non-English speakers in the room and know how to deal with it. Japanese tourists will often watch comedy shows out of cultural interest, the same way as a tourist in Tokyo might go and watch sumo wrestling. They might not be able to follow what is going on but they will sit happily and respectfully in your show for the duration. You can't let this put you off as a performer and you certainly shouldn't have cause to be frustrated at their lack of laughter. They are there, they have every right to be, so be nice to them.

In fact, this is also good advice for any audience member who is being respectful but not giving you the reaction you want or expect. Be nice to them, it may not be their fault if they don't get it.

TRANSPORTING PROPS

Suitcases or flight cases with wheels are the method most performers opt for. However, you need to bear in mind that the pavements of Edinburgh are very uneven and the landscape has a quirk of making it appear that everywhere is uphill. Whatever you decide to use needs to be a decent build quality – in 2011 the handle of the cabin bag I used to transport a computer and other devices for my show around seized up and would no longer drop down – not the end of the world but inconvenient nonetheless.

PROP TRANSPORTATION HINTS AND TIPS

* Keep a refuse sack in a pocket inside your suitcase, it frequently rains in Edinburgh and suitcases have a lot of surface area and water can seep in. If you're transporting electrical items around you need to stop them from getting wet.

* Regularly check the wheels on your case for obstructions, such as, tiny stones. A jammed wheel can wear down very quickly and you are no longer wheeling something around, you are dragging it and that can lead to muscle and back pain.

PROP DISPOSAL

If you're not going to take all your props back home when you've finished you need to work out a way of disposing of the items yourself. Venues charge a fee for disposing items left behind after the festival and it's a silly way to incur extra cost.

PROP HIRE AND PURCHASE

Rather than hire equipment for the full run some performers, in an attempt to reduce costs, have attempted to buy and sell items on eBay. It depends what the item is as to how successful this might be. In 2011 I tried to buy a used projector screen from the Edinburgh area. I think too many other performers were trying to do the same thing. When I checked in June there had been loads available, in July none were to be found.

In 2010 James Sherwood successfully bought and sold a piano for his show. The overall cost was less than the hire fee for a month. The only downside to this approach is that if a problem arises with the equipment during the run you're liable for the repair.

PROPS HINTS AND TIPS

* Be wary of borrowing anything that belongs to the venue for your show. In 2005 a show at the Assembly borrowed an empty crate from a storage room in the venue to use as a table in their production. When the venue became aware of this they sent them an invoice for £50 hire fee – plus VAT.

PROS AND CONS OF HIRING EQUIPMENT

PRO: A hire company has to make sure that items are serviceable; should an item breakdown they will have to send out a working replacement.

CON: If the item breaks down at a weekend it might take a few days before the company can realistically get a replacement to you. You need to make sure you can do the show without certain props if anything goes wrong. Cancelling performances means loss of revenue.

PROS AND CONS OF BUYING EQUIPMENT

PRO: Brand new equipment is less likely to break down.

CON: New equipment can be expensive.

PRO: Used items are cheaper and if it's a short period between buying and selling, the resale price should be close to purchase price.

CON: Used items may break down if the seller hasn't been honest about how much use the item has had in the past. If you purchase the item from eBay you might be able to get a full refund however this will leave you without a replacement and if you can't perform your show without the equipment you won't be able to recover your loss of earnings.

UNWANTED VIDEO RECORDERS

In 2008 Alex Petty from the Laughing Horse sent an email to everyone doing a Free Festival show informing them about an individual[9] who would try to film shows without asking for the performers,' venue owners' or anyone's permission. In the past he'd become aggressive when he was asked to stop and had to be forcibly ejected from at least one venue. He was not accredited by the Fringe office and after the Fringe rejected his accreditation, as his company appeared to be phony, they were subjected to a stream of abusive emails and threats.

---

[9] For some reason I Googled the guy's name while I was putting this book together and discovered that he was issued a Civil Restraint Order in 2010, which prevents him from issuing claims or making applications in all county courts in England and Wales and in the High Court. These orders are usually given out when a number of court claims or applications have been dismissed or struck out for being totally without merit.

More than anything no one could understand what he wanted the footage for. Fringe venues don't have anywhere near the lighting levels needed for a decent quality video recording and without access to the sound desk the only sound recording could be made through a microphone on the camera meaning all sorts of background and audience noise would be picked up. On one internet forum a user said they had discovered video recordings of themselves performing stand-up at a Fringe venue on an unknown website. The videos had a copyright notice at the beginning proclaiming the material to be the property of the cameraman and website. However it was unclear how they had found this site in the first place and as they hadn't included any links to it wasn't possible to verify their claims. Assuming this was true then the video may have been an attempt to add some content to the site in order to sell advertising space.

As a performer it's worth knowing your position with regard being videoed during a show. For someone to record in a private place they need permission from the building's owner. If they get permission to record then the copyright of the recording would belong to the camera operator. However, they can't legally distribute the recording either through YouTube or DVD without a written release from the performer. By signing a release form you're potentially signing over the rights to the material included in the recording, depending on the small print of the release form.

Recordings of you made in public, on the Royal Mile for example, don't require a release as the recording was made in public.

This issue is starting to come up more regularly with the increase in smart phone users videoing concerts and shows on these devices. Most of these people aren't actually aware they're doing anything you might not want them to do.

In 2009 I got on stage to do a short set in a compilation show and discovered someone in the front row of the crowd with a full sized camcorder. Evidently they'd been recording the entire show up to that point. When I asked them to put the camera down, they refused. When I asked them who had given them permission to film the show, they said no one. I asked a second time and then told them if they didn't put the camera down the show wouldn't carry on. They eventually put the camera down but clearly weren't happy.

This understandably put an atmosphere in the room and to alleviate this I had to explain to the audience that most of the acts were signing on or in the country illegally; videos of them might be a bit inconvenient. A couple of minutes of standing my ground while I did some material and everyone was back on side.

The person running the show spoke to the amateur film-maker afterwards and apparently they'd only bought the camera a few days ago, were filming for fun and were planning on putting all the shows they saw at the Fringe on YouTube. Asking whether or not that was something the performers wanted them to do had never occurred to them.

I suspect this problem may have arisen due to the venue being a free venue. Audiences assume that because the ticket is free it means they can do anything they want. Paid venues have more notices up about not recording shows and venue staff are on hand to deal with the situation when it arises so the performers don't have to.

Appearing in as many showcases as possible during the Fringe is a good way to market your show. It allows you to flyer people who have just seen you be funny and they're more likely to take your flyer and come and see your show. Just because your show might be in a paid venue doesn't mean you won't perform in one of the free shows at some point during the festival. Poorly lit, badly recorded film on the internet of you having a difficult gig could put off potential clients or agents from booking you later in the year.

FREE VENUE SPECIFIC SHOW MANAGEMENT

If you're planning on being in a paid venue the following information is not relevant.

GET AN ASSISTANT

Paid venues have staff on hand to act as front of house manager, making sure the audience find the room and sit themselves in roughly the same area. Free shows don't have any staff at all so I recommend getting someone to do this stuff for you so you can concentrate on mentally preparing for your show.

RUN-IN MUSIC

In 'The Great Big Comedy Picnic' we use a run-in CD. This is a ten minute CD we start 10 minutes before start time, which announces "10 minutes till show time", "5 minutes to show time", "2 minutes to show time" over up-beat music and then finally plays in the Pearl and Dean music to indicate the start of the show. This is the easiest way to let the audience know what's going on and let them prepare for the show to start.

On days when we've had CD problems and not been able to play the music before the show the audiences are noticeably colder at the beginning and take longer to warm up. The music in the background can set the scene for the advent of a show and gives an air of professionalism to the whole thing. Shows where the performer just wanders in at the start time, shuffles on to the stage and just starts talking rarely get good write-ups. Run-in CDs are easy to make and you can easily mix tracks together in Audacity.

Comedians often have their own favourite tracks on their run-in CD that they use to get them into the mood for the show. Choose music which is in keeping with the show that's coming and that you'd like to hear twenty or so times on consecutive days.

SHOW MANAGEMENT HINTS AND TIPS

* On CD make your run-in music all one track. DJ decks have a single play option that conveniently plays one track and then stops. You can set your music running and then get on with preparing for the show.

* On MP3 or Smartphone devices make sure you use a music player app that uses a playlist, with a play once setting.

TIMEKEEPING

You need to start on time and shouldn't be tempted to try to steal punters from other shows by guiding people into your show rather than the one they came to see. I've seen this happen loads of times, performers walking up to lost looking punters and asking "are you looking for the comedy?" then pointing people into their show instead of the one they wanted to see. Start times in the Free Festival are staggered to stop this from happening. If you're doing this it means you're starting late and any punters you do have in won't be pleased you've left them sitting there for 15 minutes while you try and round up a bigger crowd. Plus the punters you trick into coming in will quite quickly work out they're in the wrong place and they'll leave. The ones you did have and kept waiting will be inclined to follow them.

FRONT OF HOUSE MANAGEMENT

As mentioned in the ushering section, front of house management is important for performers. Audiences that are spread out across a big room don't laugh as much as they do when they are seated next to each other. Someone needs to move them so as they are sitting together and near the front.

Option 1. Simply stand by the door, say hello to people on the way in, make sure they're in the right show and then ask them to sit in the front rows.

Pro: It's cheap and requires no planning.

Con: You don't have any mental preparation time before your show starts to think about the beginning of the show.

Con: You actually have to have pretty good people skills to ask people to move from where they've positioned themselves. People take offence at anything and if you get distracted when they're walking in and you miss saying hello to someone they might think they've been snubbed. Or they might not like the way you asked them to move and when the show starts they're feeling hostile towards you.

Con: There is no impact at the beginning of your show. You only get one chance to make a first impression and when the audience catch sight of the performer before the show starts it's anticlimactic. This is theatre and you should use every trick you can to help make the show go better. If you go and watch a play the theatre staff will give you an announcement that the show is two minutes away from starting, then two minutes later they drop the house lights – so as the room is dark – and simultaneously bring up the stage lighting and raise the curtain.

Option 2. Get someone else to do all this for you.

Con. It costs money and requires planning.

Pro. Frees you up before your show starts to set-up props and computers. Also allows you to pace around backstage getting ready for the start of the show.

Pro. Audiences are usually in the right place when the show starts and pointing in the right direction.

Pro. Takes the pressure off you and gives you someone to talk to after the show.

LATECOMERS

We've all been late for something. It's perfectly natural. In free shows you have two types of latecomers. Firstly there are those that were planning on coming to watch your show but got stuck in traffic, were held up at another show or simply couldn't find the venue.

The second type of latecomer is one that turned up outside the venue one minute ago, looked at the board with all the shows on, saw your show title and decided to themselves "I've only missed the first quarter of an hour, I'll go and see what it's like." Now that might not seem like a bad thing but unfortunately these types of latecomers can cause you problems. In my shows over the last few years these types of latecomers have caused disturbances lurking in the doorway or in front of the stage while they decide whether or not to stay, they've moved furniture around so as not to sit with the rest of the audience, finished off phone conversations in the performance space, had lengthy and loud discussions on where they were going to sit, whether or not they're in the right show and if they're going to get a drink from the bar. They also make a lot of noise taking off coats and shaking umbrellas and then either decide to leave after a few minutes – mainly due to the fact they're not following what is going on having missed the opening of the show, or they duck out a few seconds before the collection bucket appears.

Do you really want people doing all these things while you're trying to perform the show you've spent a year working on? As an audience member would you want to be distracted from a show you're enjoying by this kind of behaviour? Aside from being generally disrespectful to the performer and the other audience members, you don't really want all this happening at dramatic moments in your plot or during your big punchlines.

My general rule of thumb is this – after the first 5 or so minutes allowing a latecomer into a free show is seldom better than refusing them entry. You can make exceptions for people who have tickets, have come to join friends or have been dying to see the show, but generally you need to find a way to keep these latecomers out.

At paid venues[10] there are late entry policies printed on the tickets, so this seems to be mainly a free show problem. How to solve it.

DEALING WITH LATECOMERS: OPTION 1

Just pull the curtain – if there is one – part way across the door way and hope that no one walks in and causes a disruption.

Pro. Doesn't cost anything, requires no planning.

Con. Latecomers walking in and out regardless causing disruptions all the way through the show.

Pro. Comics can get an easy laugh having a dig the first

---

[10] In 2012 Chris Stokes – performing at the Pleasance – received abuse via Twitter after some audience members had been refused entry to his show by Pleasance staff fifteen minutes after start time. People are weird.

latecomer that walks in.

Con. You can only surprise people once and after you've got a laugh off one latecomer you're unlikely to be able to repeat that magic. Going off script every few minutes makes for a pretty tedious show for the audience. It's also pretty pointless if you've spent a long time writing a script to keep ditching it every few minutes. The performers who say they like this as it gives them chance to engage in banter with the latecomers are the ones who clearly don't have enough material to fill the hour.

DEALING WITH LATECOMERS: OPTION 2

Get someone to sit outside your show asking latecomers not to come in, ideally the same person who ushers for you.

Con. Costs money and requires planning.

Pro. Cuts down on the amount of transients walking through your show.

Pro. Takes pressure off you, allows you to concentrate on performing the show that you've written.

In 2016 I paid my £10 a day – not bad for an hour and fifteen minutes work. Considering he spent most of the time sitting on a chair using the venues wi-fi.

CASE STUDY: FRIDAY NIGHT DRUNKS

One year on the last Friday of the festival with two days to go before it finished, one of the performers got barred from their venue after getting into a fight with heckler. That was the management's terms to describe the incident. In actual fact the person who the performer got into a fight with hadn't been in their audience at all. The man had been drinking in the bar and had been dared by his drinking partners to go into the show just to shout some abuse at the performer and then walk back out. These disruptions happened a few times before the performer finally lost their temper and followed the heckler back out in to the bar to tell them not to come back in again. This confrontation led to the usual bravado that follows when people have been drinking, the management were called and the heckler was escorted off the premises; a few moments after he'd thrown a drink over the performer.

The heckler's girlfriend, however, remained in the building and proceeded to verbally abuse the performer for getting her boyfriend thrown out. The performer eventually lost their temper, picked up her drink and threw it all over her in an attempt at instant karma. The entire incident was recorded on CCTV and the management had no choice but to bar the performer from the venue. Despite the performer being an innocent victim up until the moment they threw a drink, any throwing of drinks is unacceptable and as a licensed premises the management were obliged to act.

If this show had used an usher on the door it's doubtful they would have persuaded this kind of troublemaker from entering the show the first time. They would, however, have been able to get the bar staff to contact one of the duty managers of the venue to come down and intervene in the situation before it happened the second time. The performer would have been able to continue performing their show rather than ending up getting banned from the venue. With only two days to go to the end of the festival this wasn't the end of the world, although show collections are usually better at weekends so they certainly lost revenue. Imagine if this had been the first weekend of the festival.

COLLECTION SPEECH

If you are performing in a free show you need to have a collection speech. Keep it simple. "this a free show, free in, not so free on the way out...", remind the punters that donations aren't compulsory and thank anyone giving you anything. If you're embarrassed about asking for a collection you can simply say that it's a contribution to PBH's Free Fringe or the Free Festival. Good patter – street performer term for a collection speech – is worth researching. Some audience members are looking for guidance in how much money to give, so light heartedly suggest you've got a headache and putting notes in would make less noise. Compare tactics with the other free shows and see what they're saying, lots of performers can give you some good ideas about how to get a decent collection.

VIOLENCE

There's the possibility violence can happen in free shows as there often aren't doormen or anyone from the venue in the performance space watching the show. As a performer you have to be careful not to inflame any situation that might arise by being overly aggressive, piss taking or sarcastic. If you've got a problem you do have to deal with it on your own. My advice is to charm your way out of the situation.

I'm not trying to worry anyone here. In seven years I can only think of one incident – in a show I was producing – where there could have been a problem and it resolved without incident. More incidents have undoubtedly occurred at 'Late'N'Live' than any other show at the Fringe and typically this one of the most expensive shows to buy a ticket for and has a lot of staff present to manage the situation.

FLYERING

You'll spend more time in Edinburgh doing this than you will spend performing your show, this might seem like a sad fact but it's true. Flyering in shopping areas, such as, Princes Street is unlikely to bring in a Fringe audience. The most effective locations to flyer in are the Royal Mile, outside your venue and inside your venue.

THE ROYAL MILE

Shortly before the Fringe begins two gates are erected on either side of the Royal Mile. In between these gates is the most popular location for people to hand out flyers.

A costume can help mark you or your flyerers out as being 'show folk' while you're on The Royal Mile. Without fail there are going to be girls in their late teens and early twenties wearing suspenders, looking cold and handing out flyers featuring rude pictures of themselves – usually because they're in some kind of student production. This may be amusing and titillating, but ultimately not everyone looks good in a corset. You might be tempted to use an eye catching costume but if you're going to do this – and it can be fun – make sure what you're doing fits in with the show you're trying to sell. One year a guy I know wore full desert camouflage and walked up and down the mile handing out flyers to anyone that asked him for one. This was mostly Japanese tourists who often asked him if they could have their picture taken with him. He was then bemused by the fact most of his audience didn't speak English. That's not good for stand-up shows. He also didn't recognise that all these people really wanted was just a photo of him and were unlikely to come and see the show.

OUTSIDE YOUR VENUE

This is where picking a venue in a busy location has its advantages because it ensures there is foot traffic on the way past. You can pick up a good percentage of your audience by strategically flyering the front of your venue 30 minutes before your show starts.

INSIDE YOUR VENUE

Exit flyering is the term used for handing out flyers to audience members who are leaving another show and is a great way to pick up people who might like to stay in the same venue. For the sake of diplomacy, ask the people whose show it is if they mind before leaping in. Under no circumstances should your exit flyering impact on the smooth running of another show.

FLYERING HINTS AND TIPS

Never go into a performance space just before a show is about to start to put out flyers. Audience members get exasperated with people handing them bits of paper all day and feel the seats in the venue should be a safe haven. An audience has made the choice to watch a show, let them sit in peace before it begins to collect their thoughts. Upsetting and annoying them isn't fair on the performers about to start their show.

HOW TO FLYER

There are three approaches to flyering:

1) Make a show of yourself somewhere public and hope people ask you for a flyer.

2) Scatter gun flyering: randomly handing out as many bits

of paper to people as possible.

3) Make personal one on one conversation and tell people to come and see your show giving them the flyer as a memento.

All shows have to flyer in one way or another. First thing you need to be aware of is that successful flyering isn't just pushing a piece of paper into a stranger's hand. You need to engage your prospective audience member somehow – conversation is the best way. It's also handy to work out your flyering patter – it's useful to have a bit of comic material you can trot out that relates to the show or answers common questions.

MAKE A SHOW OF YOURSELF

The girls in stockings and skimpy outfits would be an example of this, as is the guy who dressed in camouflage gear. It rarely works well. You might be memorable as the person who looked nice or was very amusing on the street but it doesn't necessarily attract an audience. This may be different if you're a musical or dance act and can literally do your show where you stand.

SCATTERGUN FLYERING

If you can get flyers into hands they'll have an effect. Eye contact is good. Not scaring people as they come near will you will also help. Putting a flyer at 'take me' level – near someone's hand – can result in the grab reflex kicking in. Ultimately, the design of your flyer is important if you're going to take this approach, your flyer needs to be pretty self-explanatory as to what the show is, or this method will only build awareness, which might not necessarily turn into audience attendance.

Most of the free shows take this approach. Both the PBH Free Fringe and Laughing Horse Free Festival produce venue timetables with all their shows in. Whilst wacky drama students and people in printed hooded tops are trying to get them to part with £8 for a ticket, getting people to take guides to free shows is a lot easier. All you have to do is explain what the Free Festival is and them hand them the booklet with one of your flyers in it. It's a great way to get bums on seats in your show and push the free shows as a whole enterprise.

At Espionage – the venue I've performed in for the last couple of years – I simply stand outside the venue waiting for people to start reading the listings board, and then engage them in conversation offering them a printed version of the chalk board they're reading. They're usually quite appreciative of them when it's raining. Some days I end up getting them into someone else's show instead of mine but once they've seen that show they often come to my show because I'd been so helpful. Over the years I've handed out all kinds of recommendations, great places to eat, drink, which shows to watch and the cheapest place locally to get a cup of tea. Salesmanship isn't always about pushing your own product. Bear in mind that some onlooker might see your behaviour and decide your show seems be as good as your helpfulness.

ONE TO ONE CONVERSATION

If you're in a paid show, you need to make sales and this is the best option for you. Technically, with this option, you're not out flyering, you're out telling people to come to your show. You need to find your audience and this involves talking to people and finding out what sort of thing they like to see. Then you tell them what your show is and recommend other things they want to see. It's simple. Don't forget each bit of paper is potentially £8 in your box office fund so you've got to be nice.

FLYERING ETIQUETTE

The best piece of advice you can get for flyering is don't be a dick. If you annoy people by trying to be wacky you'll just alienate them. If you're too pushy you'll also alienate them. If you're trying to be ironic by sarcastically suggesting "the show is rubbish I wouldn't bother watching it" you're just wasting your time and you may accidentally be revealing the truth.

Listen to what people are asking you, answer their questions truthfully and honestly and talk to them, not at them. On one night of the festival I nipped into a venue to ask them if they had a venue map somewhere as I was trying to find a venue to watch a specific show. The guy flyering out front answered me with "don't bother with that show it's rubbish; come and watch ours, it's much better." I'd never mentioned which show I was going to see. Guess whose show I went to watch and which one I didn't go anywhere near for the rest of the festival.

In Edinburgh there are Fringe-goers everywhere. You can stand outside a show that's similar to yours and hand out flyers to people who are leaving it, or waiting to go into it; you've got a great set of possible audience members right there.

ANNOYING TACTICS

1) Walking down the royal mile in slow motion – who tells drama students to do this? Has anyone in history ever said *"oh they're walking in slow motion....let's go and see that."*

2) Forming a tableaux[11] with flyers in hands – like people will want to take them because you look like a picture.

---

[11] A representation of a picture, statue, scene, etc., by one or more persons suitably costumed and posed.

3) Forming a tableaux where you're all lying on the floor like you're dead, or just lying on the floor pretending to be dead. Unless your show is about the song by L7 in which case I'll let you have that.

4) Chasing someone up the street who's declined your flyer trying to push a flyer in their face.

In my opinion the single most annoying tactic I've ever seen was a group moving along the Royal Mile in slow motion pretending to hand out invisible flyers. What a bunch of ****s!

ASHLEY FRIEZE'S ADVICE

I've known Ashley since 2003 and without doubt he's the best performer I know at handing out flyers. Most comics I know hate flyering whereas Ashley seems to enjoy it. This might well be the secret to it. Here is his advice.

"I've been handing out flyers at the Fringe since 2004. That year I was flyering for a paid show I was performing and producing and I really needed to 'close the deal' when I gave out a flyer to make sure we didn't lose our shirts on the show. Each flyer was potentially worth £6 to us so when there is that kind pressure to get bums on seats, you learn a few tricks.

You can go round the tables at a venue, or a pub near a venue, and see if people are show watching. At the world's largest arts festival people kind of expect to have some approach made to them regarding shows. If they say no, simply move on. I sometimes comically put the rejected flyer to the back of the pack to have a good think about what it's done, smile at the next person as if to say "ah well" and then start again. Bear in mind, if you're flyering a queue or gathering that everyone can see you and your behaviour, and will decide based on how you treat people whether or not to say yes or no.

No matter how much crap you get from the potential recipients of your flyers, no matter how desperate you feel, no matter how unfair it seems or how down you are, DO NOT take it out on the punters through doing something stupid or being unpleasant to them. If you do then nobody will take your flyers and you'll make it harder for everyone else who is flyering in that vicinity.

Flyering is about selling your show and you can easily get into the 'Chugger' – charity mugger – frame of mind where you're reeling off a script no longer knowing what the words mean and being told to sod off a lot. This is where you need to stop, take time out, think about how to explain your show to people without using the same words as before. Get into your happy place and start again. I like to tell people to come and see a show I believe in. If you can't do that, then take a break until you can."

FLYERING HINTS AND TIPS

* Don't bother swapping flyers with the other flyerers, you're not going to watch their show, and they won't come to yours: it's a waste of paper.

* Have flyers! One year, a show's selling point was that it was more environmentally friendly than other shows as it didn't use flyers. It might have been better for the environment but they didn't get much of an audience.

* Be respectful of other flyerers. If someone is having a chat with a prospective punter don't butt in offering one of your flyers, the chances are the prospective punter then won't come to either show.

* Be respectful of other shows. Don't ever walk into a room with a show in progress and start handing out your flyers. You would think I wouldn't need to say this but it happens every year.

* Minimum 90 minutes flyering a day. Be nice and go and give people lots of pieces of coloured paper.

* Shows with a bigger cast should make a rota where everyone covers a certain number of flyering hours per day. Either in staggered shifts at the same location or simultaneously at different locations.

SPRING DAY'S FRINGE TIP

"The next time I buy a jacket the deciding factor is going to be whether or not I can get flyers in and out of the pockets.......I was trying to flyer this one guy and as I pulled one out the pockets which were too tight, the zip scratched my hand. I'll never forget the look on that guy's face as I tried to hand him a piece of paper from what was very clearly a bleeding hand."

THE MOST IMPORTANT PIECE OF ADVICE FOR SURVIVING THE FRINGE

You have to pace yourself. It's the only way to survive it. You can't be drunk every night, it's too expensive and you end up tired all the time and on auto pilot through your shows, which isn't the reason you're up there. Either you're at the Fringe to get better as a performer – not to scrape your way through it a physical and mental wreck – or you're there to be discovered by a TV producer as a fresh new face, and faces with hangovers don't usually look that fresh in my experience. You need to look after yourself, so decent accommodation is a necessity.

ACCOMMODATION

You need to rent either a room or share a flat with others. There are no two ways about it. I've seen people attempt to beat the system by using campsites or camper vans. I myself ended up staying in a hostel for the duration of the 2003 Fringe. It was awful. You're in a room full of farting and snoring and the shower is the most amount of privacy you have. You need somewhere where you can relax and unwind before bed, somewhere you can go back to for an early night, somewhere to just sit in front of a TV and watch crap for half an hour or chat with friends. Having these things will help keep you sane.

First timers are often tempted by the idea of campsites as they appear cheaper and require less organisation. In Edinburgh the campsites are miles away from the Fringe area. During the daytime you have to use public transport to get to and from them and at night, once the buses have stopped running, you have to get a taxi back. Plus if you have to hang around in coffee shops all evening between shows you're going to be paying coffee shop prices for a drink. These costs soon add up and end up costing more, on a night per night basis, than sorting out a flat share.

As for the weather, it's Scotland and rain is inevitable. If your tent springs a leak and everything you own is in there, you're going to have problems. I've had every weather eventuality during the Fringe from heatwaves to summers of nothing but rain. Others have tried living in a van for nearly a month, which is quite simply dirty and unpleasant. Aside from it being a month of using public toilets, you also have to find a swimming pool or gym you can go to just to use a shower and you'll have to keep moving the vehicle due to the strict parking regulations in Edinburgh.

In 2009 I let a guy who lived in a small camper for a month use the shower in my flat, which he really appreciated. By week three of the Fringe he was in a terrible state, exhausted and demoralised, mainly because he wasn't able to ever just go back to his van for a sit down with a cup of tea and to listen to his own thoughts. The first evening he used our shower he was in and out of the flat in about an hour, he used the bathroom and then sat and had a cup of tea. By the end of the week he was there for two hours at least. He was finding the lack of companionship difficult. Living on your own in a van isn't easy and it certainly isn't relaxing.

HISTORY OF MY EDINBURGH ACCOMMODATION

2003

I wasn't supposed to be in Edinburgh for the whole month in 2003. I was only supposed to be there for the first twelve days. Arranging a flat share proved to be difficult as other performers that week were going to stay on a campsite or staying with friends in Edinburgh. I selected the Castle Rock hostel for those nights and booked and paid for my stay around June. It's important to book early during the festival season. Cost was £13 per night with no food included. When it became apparent I had to stay longer, as the staff at my venue weren't comfortable with someone else taking over the running of the show on my exit, extending my stay at the hostel was the easiest option.

In the end, I spent around twenty eight days there. I'd rise at 10am, leave without breakfast, pick up something to eat on the way to my venue, collect flyers from the print store, hand them out for about three hours, have lunch, return to the hostel in the afternoon for a shower, do the show, and then go and watch other shows and hang around bars with other comics. I'd return to the hostel late at night, use the internet terminal, write my journal of the day and then go to bed around 2 to 3am.

I'd never stayed in a hostel before, so the first thing that I discovered was just how much burping, snoring and farting goes on during the night and how smelly strangers' feet can be. By the second night I'd bought myself earplugs and discovered the merits of keeping windows open all night.

The first thing to take its toll on you in a hostel is the general lack of privacy. The bedding is changed for you on a regular basis but the mattresses are a bit crappy. What surprised me most was the fact there was a large community of long-term guests in the hostel and I discovered at the end of my stay that I was unpopular with them. Evidently never spending any time in the hostel at all alienated the 'inmates,' which I found odd since my favourite type of flatmate is one that's never in. They apparently felt I was snubbing them and didn't want to get to know them.

Based on this experience, the memory of how my back felt after twenty eight nights on a rubbish mattress, the lack of privacy and the fact my favourite shirt went into the laundry and was never seen again, I have to conclude this wasn't a great way to live for a month and is not something I would recommend. No disrespect to the Castle Rock hostel, I've stayed in there on occasions since then as it's a cheap and convenient place to spend a couple of nights. I just wouldn't stay there for that long again. If you're only at the Fringe for a week and have stayed in hostels before, then maybe it's worth considering.

2004 and 2005

Eight of us shared a student flat with four single beds. Four sets of keys were supplied to us and we were prohibited from having copies cut.

One shower and the lack of hot water on demand soon became a problem. I gave up on having a shower in the flat and used the showers at the swimming baths I went to each day – an exercise routine can be important to maintaining a fitness level to get you through the whole thing. My girlfriend set an alarm to get up before everyone else and be the first one in the shower. One flatmate was more creative and worked out how to lock the shower door from the outside preventing anyone else from using it whilst he waited twenty minutes for the turbo boost mode on the immersion heater to do its job.

Total cost was £2400 for the month. Divided by eight it equalled £300 each. £75 per week which was not to be sniffed at, but I don't think I'd do it again. The students we legally sublet the flat from were also a bit miffed when they got the electricity bill, it seems using the turbo boost mode on the hot water heater six times a day had really cut into their profit margin.

2006

We moved to a four double bedroom flat with two bathrooms, and it was great. I paid about £450 for the month. This was for a flat close enough to the Fringe action to walk back to without the need for buses or taxis. I shared a room with my girlfriend who also paid £450. On a cost per night basis this works out at around £15 per night. Only slightly more expensive than a hostel but considerably more comfortable. We returned to this flat the following three years.

Our only problem with the flat was that the landlady insisted on a thorough clean after we'd left, which was a one-way street, since the flat was provided to us in less than pristine condition. Holiday-let accommodation – short term rental of a month or so – should come with an expectation that you should do some tidying, but you shouldn't be risking your deposit on having to do a deep enough clean of the bathroom.

2009

We moved a short distance to a smaller flat with one less bedroom and one less bathroom. I found this new flat through a letting agent. Which in itself was a really time consuming process. I'd been in email contact with around sixty different people during this process trying to find somewhere. Potential landlords aren't very forthcoming with the address or the postcode when they know their property isn't conveniently located. A number of properties described as being a short distance from the Pleasance or Gilded Balloon, were in fact a short distance by car. As a general rule of thumb the cheaper the rent the further it's located from the Fringe action. Some landlords were just blatant time wasters deliberately not supplying postcodes, two emails later and I'd find out they were asking in excess of £3000 for a property located miles away from where I needed to be.

One landlord contacted me about a property on the Royal Mile asking for £7000 for a three bedroom flat, out of courtesy I replied thanking her for getting in touch, but explained that was out of our price range. Two days later I got a reply to this email, telling me it wasn't out of every theatre companies price range and she'd just let it for £7500. To this day I've still no idea why she bothered sending me this email.

Cost wise my rent increased slightly to £483. However this was for a more comfortable flat that came with Wi-Fi, digital TV and a washer dryer. Gas and electric were also included in the price and I'd certainly had to kick in £20 towards that in previous years. Those electric showers use a lot of juice.

In the following years, we've been back to that property and negotiated directly with the landlord, saving her the agency fee. This saving has in turn been passed on to us, and the rent has been cheaper. My cost for 2010 was £400. If we'd left the place in a mess I doubt she'd have been happy renting the place to us again.

ACCOMMODATION HINTS AND TIPS

* The optimum number of rooms to make renting cheaper is four double bedrooms, but make sure the property has two bathrooms and two toilets.

* If the property is described as "sleeps six", check how

many bedrooms it actually has. Landlords will stick a bed in the lounge and call it a bedroom. This might bring the rent down but without a living room there is no place to relax and if the kitchen is small you might not have anywhere other than your bedroom to sit and eat a meal.

* Check that the hot water is instant. People will want to get up and out in the mornings and if they have wait after each person has used the shower for more hot water, tension is going to build up. Electric showers heat water as it's used and can be the most convenient.

* Harmony in your flat is important. You might want to consider whether you have shared motivations with the people in your flat. If you want to party while they want to rest and tighten up their show for tomorrow, it's going to get messy.

* Flatmates who are there for the full run are easier to live with. Guests who are there for a week usually go out partying every night and therefore have a tendency to make noise when they come in. They're also very good at leaving you with cleaning and washing up to do after they've gone.

* Check to make sure gas and electric are included in the price. In 2006, not only did we have extra expense from our surprise of the Pay As You Go meter, but also the hassle of having to send someone to do the top-up.

* Beware that a number of fraudsters operate on sites like Gumtree offering to let property at lower prices. They will want upfront payment of the rent via a money transfer service. Ask for proof of ownership and use search engines to check to see if they have just copied the details from the legitimate landlord[12].

* If people do want to party, the flat is actually one of the

---

[12] James Sherwood brought this con to light

worst places in the city to do it. Outside there is a festival going on with bars open until 5am.

* If you're going to have people crashing in your lounge for a night here and there, make sure everyone in the flat is aware and doesn't have a problem with it. One flat mate had different friends staying every night one year, it can lead to a lot of tension when there is a constant stream of strangers passing through and people have valuables in their rooms.

* If you were happy with your flat and you think you might like to return, invent a reason to speak to the landlord in the last few days of the festival. I contacted the letting agent on the last day of the festival to ask if I could keep my car on the car park until 6pm. The agent was too busy to ring the landlord themselves so passed along the landlord's phone number. I kept her details and contacted her the following February. Maybe tell the agent you've got a loose door handle, ask how much cleaning you need to do before you leave or ask where new bags for the hoover are, anything to sneak the number from them.

LESSONS LEARNT

The Edinburgh flat should be a safe haven away from the Fringe. You may end up talking about how it's going 'out there,' but it makes sense to keep the flat as a place where you take a break from everything. Landlords are quite money-grabbing with their tenancy agreements – and it's a sellers' market. Treating the flat with respect is a good way to get your deposit back.

The Fringe is definitely a marathon and if you overdo it everywhere, you'll soon lose your energy, voice and general well-being. Your flat can be a good place to recharge.

One good bit of advice is choose flatmates carefully. They

should be chosen on the strength of whether they're going to be easy to live with, rather than any other criteria. When we've talked about new flatmates I've gradually noticed questions creeping in that I never dreamed I'd ask before, "have you been to their home?...was it tidy?....was there any washing up waiting to be done?"

Agree to a few things up front like how much you'll spend on hand wash, toilet roll, and other necessities and work out who'll buy milk and when. Make sure everyone knows that when they leave, their rooms have to be tidy, hoovered, rubbish removed and surfaces wiped down.

FLAT SHARE HORROR STORIES

I heard one story about a guy sleeping on the sofa in someone's flat sited near the kitchen. One of the other tenants had a habit of raiding the fridge in the middle of the night, naked, and they would often awake and be greeted by the sight of a man's bits illuminated solely by fridge light.

In 2004 we had a problem with one visitor – not even someone who was paying rent – who smoked something overly powerful being passed around the flat and became not only sick but massively paranoid and proceeded to lock themselves in the toilet for two hours. Thankfully the toilet was separate from the shower so he wasn't stopping anyone from using that.

The same overly powerful substance was most likely the reason another occupant – who was quite frankly on the edge anyway – pinned someone up against a wall in the lounge and threatened to cut their throat with a sharp kitchen knife. I wasn't in the flat for that incident but upon hearing about it I did think "next year I would like the flat to be a little bit quieter."

MISCELLANEOUS TRAVEL INFORMATION

Finding Scotland is quite easy, as is finding the capital city. There are a few ways to get there, each with its pros and cons.

CAR

If you have props, or can share driving and fuel costs, this is by far the easiest way to get to Edinburgh – your schedule, your space. Edinburgh is, however, quite a long way from most of the UK. You also need to pick a good time to leave if you are driving back on the English Bank Holiday otherwise you'll spend most of the trip in a traffic jam. Tens of thousands of people will also be returning from places, such as, the Lake District and Blackpool. I usually leave at about 6ish on the bank holiday and arrive back in Manchester around midnight.

PARKING

Most properties only come with one parking space, if that. On-street parking in Edinburgh is highly regulated and metered between 8:30am and 6:30pm. Most performers who arrive in their cars usually drive outside of the controlled zone and then, much to the annoyance of the residents, find a quiet street to park on, and periodically go back to check it still has windows and wheels.

TRAIN

Despite the festival being on there isn't an increase in trains going to Edinburgh during the season and in some cases they don't even add any extra carriages. If you're planning to go by rail, you need to book a train ticket as soon as they become available. Also, don't assume just because you booked a seat you're actually going to get to sit down, this is UK rail we're talking about. Finally, expect the carriage to be full of drama students, noisily making their way up to the Fringe too.

In 2006 I boarded the train at Manchester Piccadilly bound for Edinburgh and by the time I'd reached Preston I had already been offered two flyers for student drama shows.

With the pressure of having a script to learn and a generally high stress level anyway, some performers pay for a first class upgrade on the way up. Not only is first class more comfortable but the access to table space and being generally less cramped means you can use the time to concentrate on your script and enjoy the ride.

AIR

Edinburgh has an international airport about ten miles outside the city with regular transport links into the centre. International visitors usually find it easier to fly directly into Edinburgh, rather than arrive further south and try to make their way there by public transport.

There are good bus links from the airport into the city centre. Car hire isn't necessary. By the time you've paid the hire fee you might as well just get a taxi. In recent years it's become more popular with performers travelling from regional airports in the UK, such as, East Midlands and Luton as it's often cheaper than the train and quicker.

COACHES

It's years since I've been on a coach to Scotland but I can't imagine it has improved much. I would expect it to be a similar experience to booking a train, possibly worse. Owing to the increased travelling time and cramped space on board, I wouldn't recommend it. You need to arrive at the Fringe ready to hit the ground running and skimping on your transport won't help. That said, if you are going to cut a little cost on transport by using the £1 'super mega bus off peak rate,' then you're best advised to do that at the end of the Fringe, rather than the beginning.

If you're contemplating the coach because you think you can do the Fringe on a shoestring budget, then it's worth a reality check. The Fringe is not cheap and if you're at risk of struggling financially, Edinburgh in August will be your downfall – see later for an example of what can happen[13]. At the Fringe, there will be unforeseen expenses, so if the coach is your way of preserving your emergency money, then good luck, but if it's the first sign that you can't afford to do the Fringe this year then you could always wait until you can afford to or take on some extra work in the meantime. I took on a bar job at The Frog and Bucket Comedy Club to pay for my 2002 and 2003 trips to the Fringe.

CASH. HOW MUCH OF IT DO YOU NEED WHILE YOU'RE THERE

I try and live on £10 per day at the Fringe. In 2003 I managed that quite easily. Since then you may have noticed there has been some problems with the world economy. Food prices have risen and £10 isn't as easy to live on as it used to be. I usually eat out once a day for convenience but stick to the cheaper outlets, such as, the Mosque Kitchen – £5 for chicken curry and rice. Everything else I try and eat in the flat. The rest goes on beverages.

The discount cards you can get for your venue are helpful but not brilliant. If you're in a free show on your own, you can keep your collection money, or if you do a guest spot in a free compilation show you might get a cut of the bucket money and this can help you out as it stops you from using cash machines. However you can't rely on having great collections every day. If you're in a paid show you might not see any money until after the festival is over.

---

[13] The Mighty Swob story later on.

You need to make sure you have enough cash on hand in your bank when you arrive to cover you for the month. £12 is a reasonable figure per day to get by on if you don't drink alcohol. To get a more accurate figure of how much you spend, keep track of what you spend at a weekend. Eat out a couple of times somewhere cheap, buy a few drinks here and there. When you work out how the average between those two days multiply it by twenty eight.

Bear in mind that if you have a lot of 'cheque to follow' gigs in September that you'll need cash to live on then as well. I know a lot big earning comics who were 'tapped out' until October, as cheques weren't following as quickly as they should have.

WHAT TO BRING WITH YOU

Obviously you need clothes and your creature comforts with you. You can pick up most items from the bargain shops and supermarkets in the city but they don't always tend to be the best value. A large sized umbrella is something you should bring with you as well as a waterproof jacket: there will be days when you have to go out on the Royal Mile flyering in the rain.

Two pairs of comfortable walking shoes are a necessity. You will be on your feet all day, so your feet need to be looked after. Arches need supporting and heels need padding. It's not uncommon to see performers on stage whose shoes don't necessarily match their outfit. Alternate your shoes each day so as they have time to dry out and don't become too smelly.

Other bits and pieces that you'll find useful to have with you include: Blu Tack, blank CDs, marker pens and a roll of gaffer tape. Keep a spare copy of your run in CD with you as they have a tendency to get misplaced. You'll also need access to a computer with a CD burner if you haven't got a laptop with a drive on it. However it's quite likely that someone with a PC will just help you out and do it for you, so keep a copy of anything you might need on a USB flash drive.

Internet terminals are available at the Fringe office and internet cafés. If you have a smart phone you can respond to emails from that. However, although the population of Edinburgh increases for the month of August, the data capacity of the network doesn't; phone services, such as, SMS and email become noticeably slower as the month goes on.

A small point and press camera is also a good thing to have in your pocket just to keep a record of the experience.

UNFORESEEN EXPENSES

Alex Petty from the Laughing Horse recently told me someone emailed him to ask what unforeseen expenses they might expect whilst doing a Fringe show. As Alex pointed out by definition unforeseen generally means you can't see it coming. That might not seem that helpful but I genuinely don't think there is any way you can answer that question. Some examples of unforeseen expenses:-

* **2011. Not the right device**

I discovered that my laptop's VGA socket wasn't the right connection for the TV screens in my venue. I had to purchase an adapter to convert VGA signal to VIDEO OUT. That device cost me £40 that was in addition to the £60 I'd spent on a projector screen and £50 hiring a projector for the month. I wasn't aware that the performance space had 5 TV screens on various walls. It clearly made more sense to use them than the projector screen as it meant everyone in the crowd had unimpaired views of the photos I was showing.

* 2011. The washer dryer

In 2011, my girlfriend put about two weeks' worth of summer clothing into the washing machine before she went out one afternoon expecting to take it out of the machine later on and put it on drying frames. What she discovered when she came back was after the wash cycle had finished, the machine had automatically switched to using the drying programme and that her delicate cotton clothing had spent ninety minutes on the highest heat setting. Her clothes had shrunk to doll size and despite two hours of soaking her clothing in cold water and then putting them on to try and stretch them back to the correct size, not everything was salvaged. She had to go and buy about a weeks' worth of clothing.

* 2005. Game show prizes

During the final part of Seymour Mace's show 'Imaginary Friends Reunited', one of the characters 'Alan Alan Alan Alan' hosted a game show. The prizes were all items from a charity shop – essentially useless crap – except for a large Leopard toy which cost about £30 in Manchester. Throughout the preview shows and the first twenty two shows at the Fringe, the winners of all the prizes stayed behind after each show – without being asked – and handed back everything to Seymour. In the 23rd show, the penultimate show, the winner of all the prizes, left, taking all of them with him, something neither of spotted until we were packing everything up about ten minutes later after the show had finished. We both went looking around the venue bars, waiting areas and outside to see if they were still around to ask if we could have the stuff back for the last show, but they were nowhere to be seen. Seymour had to go around all the charity shops in Edinburgh the next day buying about twenty five new crap prizes and another full sized Leopard toy which in Edinburgh cost about £60.

FRINGE FLU

You'll get some sort of cold at some point. My girlfriend reckons First Defence is helpful at warding off colds but it never really worked for me. Other people consume Berocca tablets every day in the hope that extra vitamins and minerals will keep their system primed to ward off any viruses.

Personally I think being in damp locations with handfuls of strangers from all over the world every day, breathing in their air for an hour is bound to result in you picking something up and there really isn't that much you can do about it. Just be aware that it will happen at some point and hope that the adrenaline can keep it at bay.

Anecdotal evidence from some suggests that sleeping in rooms with open windows can help you fight off colds and flu.

FUN

Have some whilst you're there. That is, after all, the whole point. You'll meet people there year after year, you'll sit and catch up with them, exchange stories, people will come back to your shows year in year out, you'll bump into people in the street and just start chatting.

There's a fine balance between taking it seriously and taking it too seriously. If you're taking it too seriously you're not going to have any fun. Don't take it seriously enough and you'll put on shambles of a show, which isn't in anyone's interest.

WRITING AND PERFORMING SECTION

There are plenty of comedy writing guides that deal with writing jokes and material and learning performance skills. There aren't any that I am aware of that deal with writing full length shows. Shows I've done in Edinburgh have picked up one to four star reviews and some have gone on to have a life after the Fringe. This section deals with how I went about writing my solo shows rather than telling you how you should write yours. These techniques might work for you, they might not. Every comic is different and has their own methods. These are some of the choices that you might have to make and things you will need to bear in mind.

THEMES

Two schools of thought on this one. Go to Edinburgh and say to everyone "this is everything funny I can think of." Shows of just one hour of straight stand-up are very common. The second school of thought is to show everyone "this is everything funny I can think of on this subject." The implication being that actually you can think of a lot more stuff than just what is in this year's show. That was how it was explained to me early on when I'd said to friends I was going to do a solo project. Looking back, I actually think there is more to it than this. I think that if you plan on your project having a life after the Fringe, for example, in broadcast format then you need a concept to hang a show on. 'The League of Gentlemen' is not just a show with random sketches in it, they're sketches in the fictional setting of Royston Vasey. 'Little Britain' has its own twisted concept of the UK, Chris Addison's shows, such as, 'The Ape That Got Lucky' and 'Civilisation' were on the subjects of evolution and the history of the world respectively. I personally find that having a theme makes the writing process easier. For a start you have stuff to research and to look at, which helps in the assembling of raw material and ideas. I think it also gives your show the chance of a life after the Fringe in another format.

For some the theme is its selling point. Shows about things that have existing fan bases, such as, 'Doctor Who,' Michael Jackson, 'Ferris Bueller's Day Off' or seminal Manchester punk band The Fall are easier to market. They already have a fan base that you can tap into through internet forums and fan clubs; enthusiasts will also help spread the word about your show for you. Physics students started turning up to 'The Butterfly Effect' – something I'd never even considered. If you're an unknown, then it can be easier to market your show on its theme rather than on your qualities as a performer.

ROAD TESTING MATERIAL

Rather than write an entire show on a word processor and try to guess how many thousand words makes up an hour, the best way to put together an hour show is to break it down into ten minute sections. You need to know if your individual jokes and theme specific material will work in front of an audience. By breaking the show down into six 10 minute blocks it becomes easier to work out a format. It is also a lot easier to get 10 minute open mic slots than it is to get full hour preview spaces.

DIRECTION

A lot of Fringe shows have a director. This can be useful as an hour-long show needs a guiding hand to make it flow well. If you have someone who can give you directorial notes, then use them – you'd be amazed how many people you might be able to find through your social network.

If you haven't the opportunity or desire to use an outsider

to direct your show, then video your rehearsals or record them in audio form and then review the recordings as critically as you can. In audio, you'll be able to review the script, the pacing and density of the material and in video you can check out your stage craft – are you being too physical or is the show too static? Are you fumbling with props or finding yourself in the wrong place at the wrong time?

A recording is a much better medium for critically examining and tightening up your show since you will not remember every nuance of a rehearsal or performance you give.

FORMATTING SHOWS

Again you have two schools of thought when it comes to formatting your show. First option is to work out a format for your show and then write material to your format. The problem with this approach is that if your format doesn't work all of your material is pretty much useless. In my opinion it's better to write a couple of hours' worth of material and then work out which material naturally follows on from each other. The format can then be changed if it doesn't work and improvements can be made as you go along. Maybe the bit originally at the beginning works better at the end, maybe the end bit works better in the middle. You're free to make changes like that if you keep the structure loose.

FORTY MINUTE LULL

The human brain has a natural drop in attention span after forty minutes. Go to watch an act on tour and you find they usually do two forty-five minute sections. This conveniently gets them around the forty minute lull because there is a break. In an hour long show you don't have this luxury so you have to factor this forty minute lull into the construction of the show. To get round this performers include tricks, such as, introducing videos, photos, different acts, different characters, something that basically changes the visual scenery to draw back the audience's attention. Some acts, particularly American comics, often only do forty minute shows anyway. Sketch shows usually manage to avoid the lull completely as they have constantly moving visual scenery anyway. Be aware of the lull and write something into the show to compensate for it.

One common trick at the forty minute lull is to change the pace of the show into a bit that's not really meant to be funny – a charming or emotional story would do it. This lets the audience simmer down so you can build them back up in the final ten minute climax.

LOCALISED REFERENCES

As explained in the opening section the majority of the audiences are from various parts of the UK, plus English speakers from Australia, the US and Canada. With that in mind you need to make sure your material doesn't contain overly localised references; for example, someone from New York probably isn't aware which parts of London are rough or posh, certain terms, such as, 'chav' and 'scally' don't mean anything to visiting Canadians and not everyone knows that 'tattie' is Scottish slang for potato. Pretend when you're writing stuff that you're going to do the show in America or Australia to avoid talking about things only locals understand.

WORD PLAY

Word play jokes based around double meanings are the basis of a lot of jokes. However audiences whose first language isn't English may struggle with them. In some ways to them it's like trying to work out a cryptic clue in a crossword. It's not that they can't do it, it just takes time, so their response isn't going to be immediate. Consider removing overly wordy jokes completely and make sure that your big hitters aren't inaccessible to people who don't have English as their first language.

PRONUNCIATION

With an audience from various locations around the globe accents can be problem. You might not think you have an accent, but you probably have a faint trace of something that takes a few moments for the audience's ear to adjust to. To get around this you need to spend some time learning to enunciate clearly and generally slow down your delivery so your crowd will be comfortable listening to you. This will be especially important if you are using a larger room where people at the back need extra time to pick up on what you're saying – not every sound system is cutting edge.

In 2003, I produced my first compilation show. As with everything you make a number of mistakes when it's your first time and in my eagerness to produce a showcase of acts that were from outside London, I put together a line-up of newish acts from the North West. What I and some of the acts didn't realise is certain parts of the North West have stronger accents than others. One act particularly struggled. The venue staff and I tried to coach him with his accent, which was clearly something he had aptitude for as he could easily do impressions of actors, but as the run went on he became even more frustrated with the situation and starting taking this out on the audience. It became obvious that he wasn't comfortable – audiences always pick up on this – and bizarrely rather than concentrate on speaking clearly, his accent became thicker. It became so pronounced people that knew him and worked with him started to struggle to understand him. He also started putting in more wordplay jokes as he went along. Over the years a few of us have discussed this bizarre occurrence and the general consensus is that it was some sort of defence mechanism kicking in. He became so scared that he wasn't going to get the audience's approval, his overly strong accent and wordplay jokes became his excuse for failure – "it's not because I'm not funny, it's because they didn't understand me". So, if you want your show to work, speak clearly and if you want an excuse for it not working, write a show entirely full of Gaelic puns.

SWEARING

Without wanting to stereotype Scottish people, swearing is something they're good at and are not remotely offended by. Other sections of the audience, however, don't always feel the same way, particularly during the daytime. Foul mouthed rants – not something I'm knocking, I enjoy a good one myself – don't always feel right during daytime shows. Daytime shows at the Fringe feel very different to night time shows which is something it's quite easy to forget, particularly when you do all of your preview shows at night.

As previously mentioned, families watch shows together and audiences become uncomfortable when people are swearing in front of children, they're also not used to hearing bad language during the daytime. Most people aren't used to watching shows during the day. Aside from the occasional matinee performance at a theatre, the common experience of watching things during daytime is TV where swearing doesn't usually take place until after the watershed. Therefore, swearing during daytime shows is more noticeable and can feel out of place, taking the audience out of the moment. As a performer you want your audience to be following what you are saying rather questioning what you have just said.

My only comparison here is 'suspension of disbelief.' When you watch a film or TV show you suspend your disbelief, you accept that Dr. House can get medical results back nearly instantly despite the fact bacterial cultures take hours to develop. You accept that in some action films bullets bounce off bullet proof vests without causing the wearer any discomfort at all. In 'King Kong' you accept that an ape could be that large, yet if he took out an iPhone you'd stop and think "where did he get that from and how does he charge it up in the jungle?" Those split seconds stop you from following the story and enjoying the show. Swearing during daytime Fringe shows can feel the same for an audience. It's a distraction from what you are saying.

MULTIMEDIA

In recent years with the introduction of more portable technology shows have increased amounts of multimedia material in them ranging from PowerPoint presentations to short films being included in the shows. Funny videos, made specifically for shows, are often used at the beginning as audience warm up before the comic gets on the stage. The biggest problem with using technology is its ability to go wrong or the performer's ability to forget to do something important like plug in their computer during the set-up.

In 2011 I forget to plug my laptop in during one performance of my photo show 'Ian Fox Exposes Himself.' The computer managed to run out of juice about three minutes from the end. There was not enough time left to plug it in, turn it on and resume the show before finishing time. It was one really annoying anticlimax for the audience and I was kicking myself all the way home.

On the first day of the show I couldn't get the images to display themselves at the correct size on the venue's TV screens. Small details in images – often the basis of the jokes – weren't large enough to be seen. These issues stop shows from working, so you have to make sure you are fully versed in how to use the equipment and set out detailed check-lists before the show to make sure you avoid making such mistakes.

THE BUTTERFLY EFFECT – 2006

I would consider this show to be my most successful professional achievement at the Fringe with decent reviews from two respected publications. I think the reviews helped me get commissioned by the BBC in 2007 to turn the show into a radio pilot. We included them in the treatment as supporting documentation of previous writing experience.

For this stand-up show, the writing process started in September 2005. The idea for a show about how events can have a knock on effect came to me when I was walking around during the Fringe. After a few days of thinking about this, I went into a bookshop and purchased a copy of 'Chaos' by James Gleik, later followed by as many other books as I could find on the subject of chaos theory. I bought an A4 sized notepad, started reading the books and making notes as I went along. I pulled out facts here and there and statements, such as, "randomness is more random than people think it is" – one of my favourite statements of all time. I added my ideas and comedic spin to these facts.

I think in shows like this the most important part of a joke is the setup, if you don't believe me go out and tell people the punchlines from some of your favourite jokes and see what happens; most new pieces of material fail because the audience has no idea what you're talking about. As a comedian I learnt that the hard way in a comedy competition, I started a seven minute set off in a BBC gig with a topical joke about a national football team who had absconded from the airport on their way home after a match. I can't remember the gag but I do remember the silence when I reached the punchline – the story had only broken about an hour or so earlier and hardly anyone in the crowd was aware of it. The same joke the next night would probably have done OK; by then more people in the crowd would have known what I was talking about. Another example of this are those times when you are talking with friends and say something they find particularly funny. You might make a note of it in your ideas book and then try out the same joke in front of a comedy club crowd only to get no response whatsoever. The failure of the joke might be down to the fact that in relaxed conversation with friends you simply caught the moment and whatever you do you won't be able to repeat it again, or it might be – and I think this is more likely – because your friends knew exactly what you were talking about and the audience didn't. In your setup in the comedy gig you didn't get the same information across to the crowd and they struggled to follow you.

Setups in themed shows give you the luxury of explaining stuff to the crowd as you go along, you educate them to your topic allowing you to set a slower tempo than in a twenty minute club set. I made the decision that in the moments when the show wasn't going to have any big laughs it was going to be interesting.

As I read the books on chaos theory I noted down bits of information and then added punchlines here and there. To illustrate this I'll include the story of how Edward Lorenz discovered the butterfly effect theory. This was a story I thought was interesting and conveniently had places that you can just add to jokes to quite easily.

THE LORENZ STORY

Lorenz was a meteorologist working on a computer program that would accurately predict the weather when he made his pioneering discovery. Specifically his long term aim was to build a machine that could control the weather. During the course of his research he was testing a program he had written to make sure its results were consistent. In science you have to prove something a number of times before it's acknowledged as fact. On days one to three of his tests he input all his data into his primitive computer from his research file, inputting all the numbers to six decimal places. On day four he absent-mindedly used a printout lying around in his office that was closer to hand. The difference between the two documents was that information on the print out was to four decimal places not six. Leaving his primitive and noisy computer, held together by bits of vacuum cleaner tube, to carry out the calculations, he retired to the canteen to await the results. Upon returning to his office three hours later these tiny differences in calculations had produced a completely different outcome to the simulations produced on days one to three. In that moment he had the realisation that the tiniest change in detail can massively affect the outcome of anything. The theory of the butterfly effect was born. Years later it would be incorporated by other scientists into chaos theory.

LORENZ STORY WITH JOKES

When I told the Lorenz story I broke it up into various sections so I could tell jokes related to what I had just mentioned. Some of which I appear to have forgotten, but parts of it went like this.

Lorenz was a meteorologist working on a computer program that would accurately predict the weather when he made his pioneering discovery. Specifically his long term aim was to build a machine that could control the weather...

"....a machine to control the weather sounds like something right out of a James Bond novel, evidently Lorenz was planning on a becoming a master criminal. Intent on world domination he'd been secretly contacting estate agents all over the world to see if any of them had any hollowed out volcanoes on their books."

During the course of his research he was testing a program he had written to make sure its results were consistent. In science you have to prove something a number of times before it's acknowledged as fact. On days one to three of his tests he input all his data into his primitive computer from his research file, inputting all the numbers to six decimal places. On day four he absent-mindedly used a printout lying around in his office that was closer to hand. The difference between the two documents was that information on the print out was to four decimal places not six. Leaving his primitive and noisy computer, held together by bits of vacuum cleaner tube, to carry out the calculations, he retired to the canteen to await the results....

"......For the fourth day in a row Lorenz, unmarried at the time, was hanging around the works canteen with nothing to do but make small talk with the ladies that worked there "....oh you make sandwiches, that's very interesting...would you like to touch me?" ...it also meant that actually at the moment of great scientific discovery Lorenz like all great discoverers wasn't actually doing anything, Archimedes was having a bath when he noticed the displacement of water and famously shouted "Eureka"...Isaac Newton was just sitting under an apple tree when an apple fell and he thought why didn't that fall upwards.....Isaac may well of been picking some funny looking mushrooms that day.....Alexander Fleming, discoverer of penicillin, famously couldn't be bothered to do the washing up and eventually noticed mould growing on dirty plates.....and this is something I often have to remind my missus of when she's having a go at me for doing nothing....yes to the untrained eye I might be sitting in the lounge in my underpants in the middle of the afternoon watching 'Diagnosis Murder' but potentially I could be seconds away from greatness."

These tiny differences in calculations had produced a completely different outcome to the simulations produced on days one to three. In that moment he had the realisation that the tiniest change in detail can massively affect the outcome of anything. The theory of the butterfly effect was born. Years later it would be incorporated by other scientists into chaos theory.....

"....History would remember Lorenz but the machine to control the weather was doomed and even more annoyingly he was going to lose his deposit on that secret hideout in South East Asia."

I jotted down pieces like this in my notepad and then tried them out in front of audiences in new material nights, such as, the 'New Stuff' night at The Comedy Store in Manchester and as many open mic gigs as I could get spots in.

BUTTERFLY EFFECT FORMAT

I used a three section format for the show.

Beginning – introduction to me, the show and subject matter including the Lorenz story.

Middle – examples of the butterfly effect in life, such as, phobias – a classic example of how events early in life can affect your behaviour later on. At that point in the show, when the crowd was warmed up enough, I'd often discover if any audience members had any phobias. The most common answer was clowns and the most unusual was cheese – turophobia according to Wikipedia.

I was interested in the idea of unpredictability and an obvious thing to look into was the people who claim to be able to predict things. I found an American website where people make psychic predictions for the coming year, most of which contained no hits – apparently the technical term used to describe an accurate prediction. I printed out pages of predictions, put them in a file and kept them near my desk. I think I read around 500 before I gave up on reading them. This was around January, throughout the year I checked American news sites, such as, CNN to see if any of them had come true. By August I'd only found three vaguely correct ones.

The first was a tornado in Illinois. Now I'm not overly familiar with the weather patterns in that area so that might have been something that happened in that area on a regular basis anyway. The prediction did not specify a date or a time. However the person that made that prediction also made about ten others, so her predictions seemed like an interesting one to stick with.

Another prediction was that Dick Cheney would leave office due to a scandal. Cheney did accidentally shoot someone whilst out duck hunting that year and under normal circumstances you would expect shooting someone to bring about the end of a career however in George W Bush's administration such things were not frowned upon.

Another prediction was that Mickey Mouse would die. Mickey is safe and well but at the Pleasance Courtyard that year there was show called 'Mickey Mouse is Dead' so out of charity I gave her that one. Threeish out of ten isn't conclusive evidence for her to be considered a legitimate psychic.

End – The final section of the show was a story. A long story taking approximately fifteen minutes to deliver about a narcoleptic chimpanzee called Dave who fell asleep every time he masturbated. The story moved from location to location starting with Dave in the jungle and a chain reaction of events involving animal smugglers, doped up postmen, adulterous couples, a law breaking Swiss psychologist and a man with a fear of beards. The final event in the story being an airliner forced to make an emergency landing in Amsterdam causing major disruption to the air traffic control network across Europe costing millions of Euros and all because one monkey touched himself in the jungle.

I couldn't really road test this bit anywhere other than the previews of the show owing to the size of the piece and the fact that once it starts you can't really stop until you get to the end.

Conclusion – something to wrap the show up and then a mention of the show's collection bucket and thanking the audience for coming.

BUTTERFLY WRITING TIME

I spent two hours a day, five days a week on the project. It's important to allow some time off in the writing process to stop yourself from going mad. I also took breaks for holidays. I struggled with this timetable. I started in September 2005, by January I was keen to try pieces of material out on audiences and drop stuff into my regular gigs. The problem was the material didn't match my regular stand-up and there weren't many places in my set where I could break off to talk about what some people find a complex subject. Initially I had hoped to break down the best jokes from the show after the Fringe and use them in my regular set, but they never really fit in. This is something to bear in mind when you're working on a theme for your show. Will you be able to use any of the stuff afterwards?

My biggest problem was that by May, when I had my first preview shows, I was already sick of it all. The material felt tired before it had even been road tested. Repeating the same script twenty five times in a row can feel like that. It's important to remember that you are there to entertain the audience; even if you're sick of repeating it, they haven't heard the material before. To paraphrase the brilliant comedian Craig Campbell[14] "smile until your teeth go dry and pretend you're saying it for the first time." It's important to remember that when you're at the Fringe. How would

---

[14] Full interview on my Wordpress site
http://theianfox.wordpress.com

you feel if you went to see one of your favourite bands and they didn't play your favourite song because they were fed up of hearing it?

One way to avoid becoming sick of your material is to find variations on the wording – effectively remixing. Nothing affects an audience more than a performer who is sharing a genuine good time with them, saying it in a way which feels fresh to them.

BUTTERFLY CONCLUSION

The main thing that sticks in my mind about the show is the feeling I used to have at the end of performing it each day. I'd get to the end, do my collection speech put on some music for the audience to listen to on the way out, thank people for coming or just smile at those trying not to make eye contact with me, the whole time thinking to myself that somehow it wasn't worth the effort that had gone into it. I got decent press in the first two days of the show, and I could have gone home after that for all the difference it made to the numbers.

Later on I got one more review from 'ThreeWeeks', giving me two stars. The main complaint seemed to be that it was just me talking about the same thing all the way through and it criticised me for finishing, what was clearly a quiet show, early at the 45 minute mark. This was an odd criticism as far as I'm concerned, *"I didn't like this show and I'm upset it didn't last longer"*.

Overall it was a successful show, but at the time I didn't appreciate that.

ONE MAN DEFECTIVE STORY

You can't mention the successes without the failures. Despite having produced shows for the previous five years and having had a good year the year before, I did nearly everything wrong with this show. Firstly being busy with the radio script for 'The Butterfly Effect' pilot, I didn't get chance to start writing the show until May. I'd made the decision not to start writing as early, but I'd left it too late to be as thorough as I should have been. After only finishing the Butterfly show in August, September felt too early to start working on the next one. I partly felt like I needed a break but I was also conscious of trying not to get fed up with the material before I even started doing previews. In retrospect there wasn't enough time to think about the show properly and get an idea of what it was going to be like.

I wanted to concentrate on writing more straight stand-up so I could use the material afterwards in my regular gigs. Originally I'd had the idea of writing a fictional detective story with jokes. This was a lot harder than I thought it was going to be, plus I could only do an impression of a fast talking hard boiled Humphrey Bogart style voice for about thirty seconds before it became annoying. The theme of the show shifted to an investigation into myself and everything I'd learned from keeping myself under surveillance. Really it was just a loose way of adapting existing stand-up jokes about things I didn't understand, things I'd done, friends and family etc. As someone once explained to me "all a writer ever really has is their thoughts and experiences." Essentially it was saying to audiences up front, "I'm just going to talk about myself for the next forty five minutes."

The show was reasonably consistent in terms of tempo and laughs. A lot of the material was road tested already and audiences seemed happy with it. I didn't think it was as interesting a show as 'The Butterfly Effect' but did think it was funnier. The only press I received was an interview with Karen Dunbar on a local radio station. Karen had seen the show, enjoyed it and said people should go and watch it. I'd like to thank her for that.

DEFECTIVE STORY FAILURES

Overall, this show was difficult for me and it felt like its potential was not fully realised. The main problem with this show was the venue – a free venue that was so far out of the Fringe area it didn't actually appear on the map in the Fringe guide. Out of twenty four shows I performed about seven or eight to a handful of people that evidently didn't include any TV producers or Hale and Pace. One day I turned up and discovered a wake being held on the floor below my show – what audience member feels like laughing after such a grim reminder of their mortality and the sight of seeing someone's grieving friends and relations. This site is no longer used as a Free Festival venue – thankfully.

The running time was also an issue. Being conscious of not having enough time to write a full show I opted for doing forty five minutes rather than an hour. I've since discovered that critics rarely review shows considerably shorter than an hour, particularly with shows listed as stand-up. The main reason being throughout the rest of the year it's possible to see comics perform thirty and forty minute sets in club gigs, which means shorter shows aren't an experience unique to the Fringe and therefore unlikely to get reviewed. I also discovered you're not eligible for the Edinburgh Comedy Award if your show has a running time of less than fifty minutes. Free shows weren't eligible for a lot of awards at the festival in 2007, though this has slowly started to change in recent years. Not that I was ever expecting to get short-listed for something like this, it's just nice to know one of the judges has been along and hated you.

As far as writing material for the show went, I found writing twenty new minutes of stand-up harder than the hour of stuff on chaos theory. I think the brief of writing an hour on a specific subject is a lot easier than assembling twenty minutes on anything. I am not sure I can understand why it's so difficult, but a lot of people seem to agree with me. This is why, in the end, a lot of the material from the show didn't make it into my regular stand-up set and I've long since forgotten pretty much most of it.

The only thing I took from the show was the introduction of photos into my performance. I used photos of my girlfriend, best friend and cat – some with black bars across the eyes to protect their identity. This was something a lot of audience members commented on and something they all seemed to like.

DEFECTIVE WRITING TIME

Not enough. One to two hours, five days a week from May onwards. Also not organised enough and not enough variety in the type of material. Following the psychic predictions for 'The Butterfly Effect' had been an interesting project and something I had no way of knowing what would happen at the end, I didn't find an equivalent for this show. Something to keep things interesting for me.

PAST REVIEWS

Spend some time reading reviews from previous festivals on sites, such as, Chortle, The Scotsman newspaper and any other broadsheet reviews you can access online. It's helpful to read the one and two star reviews to try and avoid making the same mistakes those performers made and to read the four and five star reviews to see what comes across to reviewers as a good show. Not because you should try and write a show just to pander to the reviewers but because often their opinion can be thought-provoking and it shows how some ideas can be interpreted.

Reviews will also give you an idea of what themes and topics have been well covered in the past and give you an idea of things to steer clear from, as Steve Bennett from

Chortle.co.uk said in an interview, "why would I want to hear more observations about Facebook unless they are hugely insightful or brilliantly original." Reading reviews will give you an idea of who critics have considered to be highly original in the past – easily their favourite trait in any performer – and I recommend trying to see those performers when they appear locally to you to give you more idea of what they are like on stage, not just on paper.

PREVIEW SHOWS

Different people have different ideas about what preview shows are supposed to be. I've heard comics more successful than myself refer to them as "prep shows" which is what I consider them to be. They're part of the learning curve of doing a show. As a writer you have to try out different bits of material to see if they work – not all of it will – in fact, statistically, most won't. You have to try out a different order for your material to find out which works best – some orders won't work as well as others. You have to try different formats – again till you find the best one. By the very nature of previews they're going to be patchy.

The problem is that a lot of people who attend your preview shows won't know what you're doing and expect everything you say to be comedy gold. That attitude is understandable in punters, they don't go to that many gigs and then when they do make the effort to go out, and it's not very good, they get disappointed or annoyed. The problem I've found is that a lot of promoters don't understand what a preview show is – some just see it as a way of putting on a show cheaper than normal. They can also take a long term view of what you're like as a comedian by the standard of your preview show. I did a preview in 2007 for a promoter who ran a few gigs at the time – I'd done a preview in 2006 which went well and I turned up at one of his venues in 2007 to do my show, only to discover that the venue had never run a comedy show before.

I've done plenty of gigs where I've been the compère or the opening act at a new venue and you can always tell these gigs apart from the others. The audience doesn't quite know how to behave, they take longer to laugh at things, they don't know not to talk during the show, often they have no idea what is going to happen and are afraid they're going to be ridiculed by the comedian. These are not easy gigs. Some promoters choose a regular closing act as their opener for a new gig to make a good impression on the crowd. Preview shows need to be done in venues that programme comedy on a regular basis and they need a comedy savvy crowd. Needless to say my preview didn't work. Neither did the following preview from a more successful comic.

As a performer during the gig I had a choice, either stop performing my show completely and move into 'stag and hen' mode, insulting them and doing regular stand-up about dildos, or continue with my show. I decided to stick to my guns. I based my choice on experiences and things I'd learnt doing other shows. In 2005 when I had a small part in Seymour Mace's show someone handed out a great piece of advice to both of us, they said *"regardless of how well the show is going someone will walk out of it at some point during the run....."* . You might have accidentally have upset them – I say accidentally as sometimes audience members think that you have just said something you didn't actually say, or they just don't like the show regardless of how well it was going *"..... it will happen at least once in twenty five shows, regardless of how mortifying it feels at the time you can't acknowledge it, just keep going."* It happened three times in 2005 in Seymour's show, we had some tricky ones where the audience just didn't go for it at all and all you can do is just keep going. If an audience doesn't like a play you are performing in you don't start rewriting it in front of them, just as singers don't start changing the words to 'My Way' if the crowd aren't going with it.

The second factor was that I was only getting £20 petrol money for the show. If the promoter had wanted a club act, he should have paid for one. Thirdly the material in the show wasn't that different to my regular material, which was quite well road tested anyway. So I stuck with the show and *'rode the lightning,'* lots of heckling and interruptions. After the gig the other comic received an apology from the promoter for the crowd not being very good. I got a talking to about what I'd done wrong – apparently I should have *"just laid into them."* Had I done that, I wouldn't have been previewing my show.

The venue was never used again for comedy – the promoter obviously decided it wasn't suitable – but the experience affected my relationship with him. I contacted him a couple of years afterwards when he was advertising on the internet for a last minute fill-in at a town I was going to be passing. He declined my offer and his email said it had been a while since he'd last seen me and he remembered the gig hadn't gone so well.

The moral here is be careful who you do previews for. Bad previews can really damage your confidence in your work and can make you look bad. You need to pick venues and promoters carefully, which is difficult since previews are increasingly hard gigs to come by.

PREVIEW SHOW HINTS AND TIPS

* 30 minute preview shows early on can be very helpful as the reduced running time means you have less stuff to learn – takes the pressure off you and gives you an idea of whether or not the concept and format are working.

* There is not really a lot of point in learning material that isn't funny, so using notes in previews and try out spots is perfectly acceptable.

* Index cards can be less obvious than a full notepad in

front of you – although you look more like you're giving a speech at a wedding rather than a stand-up comic.

* Music stands are also a good way of disguising the fact you are using notes. Print everything up on A4 paper in bullet point form and large print so you can read it easily from a distance – and in areas of the stage that may be poorly lit – without interrupting the flow of the show. Also make sure you number the pages in case you drop them and they end up in a different order. When I say "drop" I mean in case someone like Dave Turquoise[15] deliberately moves the order of them around before the show starts and you don't notice until you're fifteen minutes into the show that you've been doing stuff in the wrong order – true story in case you hadn't already worked that one out and I'm still upset.

* Laptops are also more discreet than a notepad. Presentation programmes have what is called 'notes or speakers mode,' which can display bullet points on screen and can be advanced by a click of the mouse or remote control.

* If you can't get a preview, organise your own. Plenty of small venues will give you their space for less than the price of a weekend of drinking yourself ill. Alternatively, you can invite people to your house or offer to do a preview at friends' parties.

* If all else fails, you can splice a preview together from video clips of you discreetly trying bits of your material during longer sets. Doing this at least gives you an accurate idea of how long the show lasts.

CRITICS AND REVIEWS

Everyone wants their show to get reviewed in Edinburgh

---

[15]If you don't know who he is, consider yourself quite lucky.

but no one wants to get a bad review. I personally never read any of my reviews whilst I'm at the Fringe.

As mentioned throughout this book, when you do twenty four shows in a row some of them go better than others. There will be shows when you think, "it would be good if someone had reviewed that." Other shows will make you let out a deep sigh and hope that nobody ever mentions it again, let alone publish a review of it for Google to remember for eternity. The rest will be somewhere in between and these are most likely the ones that actually get reviewed. It is perfectly respectable to get three stars[16] for your show and this is what you should be measuring your success by, especially for your first few years. Three stars means it's a perfectly enjoyable show, if you get more than that then celebrate by patting yourself on the back – being careful not to pull a muscle, treat yourself to a doughnut or a victory lap and then go back to work and make the show better for the next performance. Sadly, I've seen people's spirits crushed because they didn't get a five star review, which is ridiculous. You have to be realistic with your expectations.

In the whole time I've been going to the festival I've only ever seen one show I would describe as a five star show and that includes shows that have won awards.

Most reviewers for the respectable publications review around four to five shows a day every day of the Fringe. That's a job I wouldn't want to do. In fairness to the reviewers they have to comment on the show that they saw. So if they turn up to a bad gig they have to base their review on what they've seen. They've got other shows to see that day and don't have the time to come back and see a show again for a second opinion. Why should they if all they are going to do is raise a two star to a three star

---

[16] Different publications have different ratings systems. For some two stars means a show is average, three is good, four is very good and five is excellent.

review?

WHAT HAPPENS WHEN YOU GET GOOD OR BAD REVIEWS?

I've had shows get four stars and I've had shows reviewed with only one star. I don't think any of them have ever made any difference to my audience numbers. The only difference I have noticed is that the shows that have four star reviews splashed all over the poster outside the venue are harder to do. I think in those shows the audience have a higher level of expectation and are therefore harder to please. They come in expecting it to be someone else's definition of good, whereas the audiences that decide for themselves that they like it, while watching the show, are usually much happier.

You would expect bad reviews to affect audience numbers but I'm not sure that they do. First of all it depends on the publication that gives you the review. Some Fringe review websites have a very small readership and you sometimes get the feeling that the reviewers are only running the sites in order to get free tickets for shows. As such I'm not sure many people really pay attention to them.

One publication worth mentioning here is 'ThreeWeeks'. It started around twelve years ago and it's a free publication in newspaper form once a week, it's also got a daily sheet and a website. The whole publication is run on a shoestring budget and mainly uses journalism students and other unpaid staff to review shows for them. Their mandate is to review every show at the Fringe.

Reviewers from 'ThreeWeeks' usually attend a show at The Stand comedy club prior to the Fringe beginning and all of them have to write up a review of the show. The editors then read each review and give feedback based on the fact they watched the same show. As far as I can see, in the case of a lot of their reviewers, this appears to be their only experience of comedy shows before the Fringe, which I don't think makes them particularly authoritative on what is and isn't a good show. Reviewers from the broadsheets and websites, such as, Chortle have been reviewing for years, sometimes watching up to seven shows at day at each Fringe in addition to reviewing a large number of shows throughout the year. Generally the more experienced the reviewer, the more worthwhile it is to read and quote their review.

Some reviewers make notes during shows and some don't. If someone is taking notes don't draw everyone's attention to it: some audiences are kind enough to get nervous on your behalf, which in turn makes them uncomfortable, which in turn stops them from enjoying the show, which stops them laughing. You really don't want a review for a show where you've made the crowd so anxious that they aren't laughing.

The issue of reviewers with notepads came up in the arts press the at the beginning of 2012[17]. By rights, they should be discreet when they're reviewing, but sadly this isn't always the case. I'd personally prefer it if they discreetly made notes during the show to avoid printing inaccurate descriptions and details. In the 2011 Fringe I emailed one publication to complain that they had wrongly identified a performer in a review. It strikes me as only fair if you're going to be overly critical of a performer then you should at least get their name right. In this case they were critical of a performer who wasn't in the show. At the time of writing the online version of the review has still not been corrected. One year a review for the 'Picnic' just referred to Ashley Frieze as a "plump, bald man" – they'd evidently not made any note of his name at all.

---

[17] Daniel Kitson complained about reviewers taking notes in his one-man show in New York and jokingly suggested members of the audience should punch anyone being that indiscreet in the head. The critics responded with a blog piece on the Guardian's website.

NOT GIVING OUT PRESS TICKETS

Believe it or not some performers have actually decided that they're no longer bothered about what critics think and don't issue any press tickets at all. In these cases it doesn't necessarily mean that the show doesn't get reviewed. Reviewers simply have to pay for a ticket as opposed to getting a free one.

In 2004 one comedian who had been selling out their shows and having some great gigs, found a two star review for their show. I'd seen the show in question – it was very well done and clearly not rubbish. The basis for the bad review was that the critic simply didn't like the performer. Now in those cases I think the critic should have just given a three star review acknowledging the show was good, just not their cup of tea. The performer's decision to stop reviewers coming in was based on the fact the show was doing good business and bad write ups could potentially damage ticket sales.

BADLY WRITTEN REVIEWS

If you receive a negative review, then bear in mind it's just someone's opinion and most people probably won't read it anyway[18]. You can also bear in mind that it may, in itself, be a badly written review. However if it's a well written but largely negative review from an experienced journalist, you may want to take note and think about what you're doing wrong. Dismissing a negative review is fair enough but you may actually be missing out on some free and constructive feedback.

There are a few things you can look for in a review which, if present, show that the reviewer hasn't done a good job.

A few examples:

---

[18] Other comedians will of course take great pleasure in telling you about it.

* Including witty comments or descriptions to liven up a write up is one thing, but making jokes at the expense of the performer or show under review is something else. Usually this indicates a reviewer who is trying to show off, rather than give a constructive critique of what they saw.

* Including a taster of the material, for example one joke from a show with nearly two hundred in it, can be really useful in giving the reader an idea of the type of humour in the show and whether it's their cup of tea. However, writing up the best jokes from the show or revealing the ending is totally different; it spoils the show for the reader should they go and see it. In these cases what they have effectively done is plagiarise your material to try and make their review a more interesting read. Should this happen to you I think it's only fair to send them an invoice for a percentage of their fee for writing the review[19].

* Focusing on one minor detail, such as, the performer's shirt, shoes or hair indicates a reviewer who didn't form an opinion on the whole show they saw. Focusing on a major detail is, obviously, different.

* Saying a show was different from what they expected is fair comment, but comparing the show to something else and saying they wanted it to be more like that suggests they went in there without an open mind. The review isn't a fair assessment of what they actually saw.

* Including derogatory descriptions of the performer's physical appearance, such as, fat or ugly, when it has no bearing on the content of the show, is highly disrespectful. If the show is about a twenty stone performer learning how to ballet dance then it's relevant but in a show of political satire it has no relevance at all.

* Getting details from the show wrong. It shows they either

---

[19]   If you do this please tell me about it www.ianfox.net email me from there

weren't paying attention or their recollection isn't great, in which case how accurate can the review be?

* Including generalised statements that can't possibly be verified. An example of this was a review I read recently that said "the show would have been better if it was on later in the day." Can anyone prove that? What relevance does that have to the show you've just seen?

* Including comments that are overly insulting and inappropriate. One review from 2011 included the line, "would I see the show again? Frankly I'd rather jam a pool cue up my urethra." Clearly that's unnecessary, specifically when you consider the show in question was a children's show. The performers quite rightly complained and the review was removed from the publication's website shortly afterwards, which would suggest those higher up the ladder disagreed with the duty editor's decision to publish it. However you can still access it through Google. The producers of the show in question were later presented with a souvenir pool cue by another performer, which they went on to use to hold up a banner advertising their show on the Royal Mile. Use all reviews to your advantage!

WHY I DON'T READ MY REVIEWS

I got my first two reviews for 'The Butterfly Effect' on the third day of the festival. I tend not to read the Fringe reviews anyway and I only knew mine existed because people started messaging me to congratulate me on them. I made the decision not to read them until I got back from the Fringe because I was concerned that even though I had good write-ups there might be some tiny detail in them I didn't particularly like and I was worried I'd end up fixating on that criticism, rather than concentrating on the rest of the show.

In 2011 when I did my show 'Ian Fox Exposes Himself' I quietly asked those around me not to tell me if they knew of any reviews for my show. Mainly because I decided that I wasn't that interested in what critics thought – either the audience like the show or they don't. I still heard about the good ones, just not through anyone in my flat. I wasn't aware until I started looking for press quotes to use for the marketing for this book that I had a couple of two star reviews I didn't know about. First one from The Scotsman newspaper written by a critic with a long history of reviewing shows. I half remember the show he saw, so I wasn't surprised it was a low star review. He had to review the show he saw and there were a couple of days when I felt the show didn't work as well as it had been doing.

The other review was one that I was glad I hadn't seen at the time. In the show I displayed photos I'd taken, images that I thought were interesting, funny or had a story behind them. Most of them were street photography shots which included some great scenes that I had just happened across, for example, walking through China Town in Manchester I noticed two strippers – wearing bathrobes – on a cigarette break standing outside the front of their club. In the centre of the city I saw some mouthy teenagers antagonising a religious enthusiast; he read passages from the bible then asked if there were any homosexuals present, to which the kids replied "yes" and proceeded to mock bum each other in front of him. At an ice cream farm in Cheshire I'd taken a photo of a lady trying to climb over an inconveniently positioned fence whilst holding an ice cream cone with a flake in it – the pose looked like the statue of liberty with a camel toe. That was the kind of thing that was in the show.

What upset me about the 'ThreeWeeks' review wasn't the fact they didn't like the show or that they had given it a low star review, or that the writer clearly used a pseudonym. It was the opening line of the review that stated the show was me displaying photos of funny things, such as, the back of my cat's head and fat people. Now there's an implication there that I was making jokes solely on people's physical attributes, which was firstly incorrect, but I felt that effectively labelled me as a playground bully with a microphone. I'm really glad I didn't see that while I was doing the show, a lot of the shots were taken in the street, some had lots of people in the images, some of the people were probably over weight, their physical appearance didn't have anything to do with the jokes in the show. If I'd started worrying whether everyone in the images had the correct body mass index and whether the jokes could be interpreted as digs at people's physical appearance, there is no way I'd have been able to concentrate on doing the show.

WHY I DON'T THINK YOU SHOULD READ YOUR REVIEWS

The saddest thing for me at the Fringe in 2011 was seeing someone I'd only met a week or so before be completely devastated by a bad review. When I met the guy on the first day or so of the Fringe he was full of beans; ten days in and he just looked miserable. His show was experimental, it clearly said that in his blurb. It was always going to be a love it or hate it thing, so there was always the possibility people weren't going to like it. His one and only review came out – a one star review from 'ThreeWeeks' – that claimed everyone in the audience left feeling uncomfortable. Now unless they got everyone to complete a survey on the way out they can not verify that statement. The final statement of the review was it seemed unlikely he'd ever get better as a performer. Unless the reviewer could see into the future I don't see how they can possibly prove that. Besides which, as someone who watched the show, I actually thought the guy had better performing skills than me. I really admire performers who can do full-on, hundred percent commitment and don't care if the crowd go with it. Does it not seem more likely that if audience members were uncomfortable that they would have just left, rather than stay to the end?

Sadly the damage was done and I don't think his confidence fully recovered, which meant his later shows weren't as good as the ones at the beginning. If you've written your show, you've worked hard on it, you know what you want it to be and your audience likes it, I don't think you should go anywhere near your reviews until the Fringe is over.

WHAT IS A BAD SHOW?

Forgetting about what reviewers think for a second we do have to acknowledge that there are bad shows out there, the question is what makes them bad shows? The simplest definition of a bad show is one where the writers and performers haven't put enough work into it. Either it works or it doesn't. No one goes up to Edinburgh with the intention of putting on a bad show. If it doesn't work it's likely to have fallen down because the material hasn't been tested enough, the script hasn't been redrafted enough, the performer doesn't know the script well enough or hasn't practised performing it enough.

Performance issues usually sort themselves out. Doing twenty four performances in a row is a good learning curve and it's perfectly natural that something gets better the more you do it. The problem is if you happen to pick up your only press review on day one of the show, when you don't know your script and are still working out teething problems. You have to hit the ground running – Rhod Gilbert had more preview shows scheduled one year than he had performances at the Fringe.

If you get a negative review in the first few days other critics might decide to go and watch something else instead of coming to your show. Critics don't like writing bad reviews. Some publications commission reviews with different word counts. Shows with three star reviews are approximately forty words, shows with four stars and above get around one hundred word reviews. Writers get paid by the word, so they'd really like to be giving shows four star reviews. They also read the other publications and if a show is getting good reviews they're more likely to follow the pack and see what they're raving about. If they're undecided about going to see a show and then see a negative review for it they're likely to choose to go and see another show.

People have varying definitions of what a bad show is. Some people just won't like your show and there's nothing you can do about that. If the majority of your audience doesn't like your show then you have problems.

WHAT MAKES A GOOD SHOW

I think a good show needs to include these two things: passion for the subject matter and a lot of hard work.

FRINGE TALES AND NIGHTMARES

THE MIGHTY SWOB

In 2003 the first year of the 'Picnic,' most of the cast were naïve about the Fringe. Some just didn't have the budget for it. The Mighty Swob was a good example of this. He and another comic, Phil Smith[20], had agreed to share a tent at a campsite for the twelve days they were at the festival. Money was already tight for Swob, but sharing the tent was going to make it affordable.

Two weeks before the Fringe started he injured his back trying to repair his 1992 Ford Sierra estate. He couldn't get the vehicle running in time to go to Edinburgh but managed to borrow a car from a friend, a 1990 two door Vauxhall Nova. For those of you not familiar with those models there is a big difference in the size of those vehicles. One of them has more than enough room for three people, three rucksacks and a large selection of camping gear in it, the other doesn't. Guess which Swob ended up with?

On the night of Monday 28th July 2003, three of us, myself, Swob and Phil Smith left the Frog and Bucket Comedy Club in Manchester at around 11pm and headed for Edinburgh. I needed to be at our Edinburgh venue by noon the following day to deliver posters for the show and to have a technical rehearsal.

We stopped at Swob's flat in Bolton on the way north to pick up his gear. We spent about an hour in the car park attaching items in black bin bags to the roof rack and trying to fit three of us, three ruck sacks and a load of camping gear into the car. The drive up the motorway was slow. The small engine struggled with the weight of three of us plus the three rucksacks and the load of camping gear, and the

---

[20] Name changed to protect the naïve.

drag from the roof rack was also a problem. In fairness to Vauxhall, I don't believe they ever claimed that the aerodynamics of a thirteen year old compact car with a load of stuff roped to the roof were great.

I don't really remember that much about the journey, I either fell asleep for some of it or I've blanked the whole ordeal out of my mind. What I do remember, however, was that we had to stop for a few hours at Tebay services, sometime around 3am, for the engine to cool down. During that time, Phil casually disclosed to us in conversation that he only had £34 to last him the first six days of the festival. Well, £31: he'd just bought himself a cup of coffee and a Kit Kat. After that he was hoping his unemployment benefit[21] – approximately £125 – was going to go into his bank account. *"That was the moment my heart sank for the first time,"* said Swob when we talked about this story recently, *"he didn't have enough money to pay for the campsite."*

Around 8am we finally arrived in Edinburgh, I delivered our posters to the venue and then we went for some breakfast at a café. Phil spent another £5. Once we'd rested and had a walk around to get our bearings we decided to go up to the Royal Mile and flyer for the show the next day. Afterwards Swob and Phil went off to their campsite and I checked into my hostel.

At the campsite Swob had a discussion with Phil about whether or not he should just cut his loses now and make his way home, but Phil was adamant he was going to stay. Between them they made the agreement that Swob would pay for the first five nights for both of them at the campsite

---

[21] Under unemployment benefit rules at the time performing at the Fringe would have been classed as work. Even though Phil wasn't likely to receive any payment for his time at the Fringe, his unemployment benefit would still have been suspended. Claiming benefit whilst performing at the Fringe could have been viewed as benefit fraud.

and then Phil would pay for the next five. After that, they would work out what to do about the remainder. In paying for two people for five nights at the campsite, Swob drastically cut into his available money.

That night it rained, which meant that the barbecue dinner Swob cooked took nearly two hours to prepare. The tent leaked and the next morning Phil declared he didn't like camping – apparently he'd never done it before. He also wasn't too keen on our first show that afternoon. The audience consisted of a lot of internationals who had no idea who the football commentators or Coronation Street actors Phil was referring to were and by 6:30pm we all knew he was going home.

I walked him to the coach station. By this point, approximately forty-three hours after we had left The Frog and Bucket, he was down to about £9 – not enough for a ticket back home and he had no other means of paying. He was also going to have to live for another four days at home on practically nothing when he got back. I stood by the gate watching him talk to the driver who took pity on him and let him on the coach without paying. Sometimes people are genuinely nice.

Other times they're genuinely ****s. At the campsite Swob explained to the manager what had happened and that he'd paid for two people for five nights, the other bloke had gone, could he either please have a refund for the four nights Phil wasn't going to be in the tent or extend his stay past the five nights he'd paid for. The answer was a decisive "No!" *"The site wasn't even that busy"* added Swob.

Swob spent the five nights on the site he'd paid for and then an extra night he hadn't paid for. On the seventh night he returned to his tent and found a note attached to it informing him he had, *"an urgent message from home waiting for him at the office."* He knew full well that no one at home knew the name of the campsite where he was staying and that no one had tried calling him on his mobile phone or any of the other numbers he'd left for them to call if there was an emergency. He figured the conversation was more likely to be about the fact they wanted money out of him. He packed up his gear, stuffed everything into the Nova and left.

For the next six nights he slept in his car parked at the Edinburgh Royal Observatory. In the mornings whilst finishing his barbecued sausage breakfast he'd drink tea and chat to the pensioners who walked their dogs there, *"they were really friendly"* said Swob *"they'd come up to me each morning, oh you're still here."* After breakfast he'd drive to just outside of the controlled parking zone where he left the car all day. He would flyer for the show, perform and see as many shows as he could get into for free. Other comedians would let him into their shows for free and friends of friends would do the same. He had a pass for our venue so he could watch all the other shows, such as, Daniel Kitson's Made Up Story, *"saw that three times and really liked it."* I'd give him tickets to things and others would happily use buy one get one free offers to get him into shows.

At night he'd go and use the shower block at the campsite he'd been evicted from, it was left unlocked and unattended at night. He'd then drive to the observatory and get stared at suspiciously by the dope smokers that go up there at night. *"Complete polar opposite of the pensioners. I would have said it would be the other way round,"* recalls Swob, *"I'd expect the affluent middle class pensioners to give me funny looks, but no, the dopers were downright hostile."* He'd try and position rucksacks and bags in the Nova to give him as level a sleeping surface as possible. At six feet one this meant, *"lying length wise with my feet by the windscreen and my head near the rear windscreen and my arse pressed up against the sunroof."*

At around 7pm Saturday 9th August, twelve days after we left The Frog and Bucket, I bid farewell to Swob at a petrol station near the Meadows. He didn't have enough cash to pay for the fuel to get home so I bought it for him and he drove back to Bolton.

He arrived in Bolton around midnight, unloaded his car, settled back into his flat and spent his first night in a bed for nearly two weeks. The following afternoon sitting in his armchair reflecting on his experience his doorbell rang. Just as he was getting up from the chair to answer it his back made *"a horrible noise"* and *"pain shot right through me"*.

"It was ten days before I stood up straight again and then a another two weeks of walking around with a stick before I was back to normal."

Reflecting on the experience now he pointed out, *"if it hadn't been for the exhaust going on that Sierra I probably would have been all right. There was enough space in the back of that car to fit in a double mattress."*

It's difficult to know what some people think sometimes. Swob and I have discussed Phil a couple of times and why he signed up for something that was going be a financial commitment when he didn't have the means in place to pay for it. Swob thinks the problem came about because of some miscommunication, *"Phil knew that people get paid to flyer for shows at the Fringe, so when he was told he'd have to do two hours flyering a day for the 'Picnic' I think he thought he was going to get paid for it and he'd get cash each day."*

Surprisingly Swob's been back to the Fringe at least four times since then appearing in 'The Great Big Comedy Picnic' and the 'Northern Monkeys' sketch show. Each time since then he has stayed in a flat.

DANNY HURST

When I first visited the Fringe in 2002 as an open spot, I performed every night in Brian Damage and Krysstal's show 'Pear Shaped at the Holyrood Tavern.' The gig itself was an institution, every comic knew it. It was the one gig at the Fringe where you were guaranteed the chance to perform. Every comic got five minutes of stage time – regardless of how famous they were, sometimes less if they were running out of time. The show started soon after midnight and went on 'til the bar shut at 3am. The comics who went there each night all got to know each other and it was a fun place to hang out.

Walking down Cowgate one evening[22], on his way to the show shortly after midnight, someone tried to mug Danny Hurst. However, things didn't go the way the mugger had expected them to. It turned out that despite Danny's short stature, he was more of a natural born brawler than his would-be attacker probably anticipated when he made the decision to mug him. The altercation didn't last long. Thirty seconds later Danny was happily back on his way to 'Pear Shaped.'

Upon arriving at the gig Danny mentioned what had just happened to one of the other comics in the crowd, put his name down for a spot in the show and joined in the fun.

A short time later two police officers arrived in the pub. Someone had seen the fight and reported that one of the men had gone into the Holyrood Tavern. The boys in blue asked a few questions and got pointed in the direction of the back room where the gig was taking place. I was sitting in the back room when I saw a police officer peer around the black cloth used as a door in the venue and look at everyone in the crowd. I saw Danny get up and go to talk

---

[22] There is some discussion about which year this story took place. So I've not included a date.

to him. Evidently they went outside to continue the conversation.

Word quickly went around the audience about what had happened and everyone was waiting to see what was going to happen next; whoever was on stage at the time was getting no attention whatsoever. A few minutes went by and Danny reappeared through the black cloth.

Apparently the police asked Danny for his side of the story. He told them he was on his way to the gig, a bloke jumped out and tried to mug him and then ended up considerably worse off for it. The officers listened to the story, said something to him along the lines of "well done" and let him go back into the gig.

Upon walking back into the show, Brian Damage introduced Danny without warning him and he took to the stage. The first words out of his mouth were, *"well....a funny thing happened to me on the way here tonight!"*

ASHLEY FRIEZE

Prior to his arrival at the Fringe in 2010, Ashley Frieze and his fiancée bought two cats. One or both of these cats brought fleas into their house, which in turn bit Ashley's legs. The bites became infected and giant angry looking lumps appeared.

When he arrived at the flat we were sharing on 13th August 2010 his legs looked horrible. The lumps had been weeping and the only comfortable item of clothing to wear were knee length shorts. Consequently, everyone could see the problem. At this point he was part way through a course of strong antibiotics that had their own side effects.

After two days at the Fringe, about ten gigs since his arrival and shortly before 21.30 16th August Ashley started to feel very unwell. Even more worryingly he went numb down one side of his body and had a racing heartbeat. He calmly approached Alex Petty from the Laughing Horse – Alex was running the show Ashley was about to compère – and told him *"I don't think I'm going to be able to do this gig, I'm going to have to go to the hospital, I'm really unwell."* Stopping only to cancel his other gig that night[23], Ashley flagged down a taxi on the street.

"The taxi ride to the hospital was slightly tense. As soon as I told the driver what the problem was, he started to panic, reassuring me – and more likely himself – that I wasn't about to go into cardiac arrest – not in his cab. In retrospect it was possibly the first taxi ride in history that definitely went the quickest route. The staff at Edinburgh Royal Infirmary were brilliant. I was looked at immediately, although that in itself was slightly worrying. As it turned out not only did my symptoms match those of a heart attack but also a stroke. I was placed on various monitors, the staff made multiple attempts at getting needles stuck in me – they were night staff and largely students with a bad aim, and then the diagnosis came in. I was dehydrated. For two hours I'd sat on a trolley in a corridor waiting for the results and re-evaluating my life. By 2am I was able to go home."

At 2:30am I was lying on the sofa of the flat I was sharing with Ashley, half asleep, half watching the TV. I hadn't turned around straight away when he walked in the room. It was only when Ashley commented *"well I've he'd had an interesting evening"* and showed me the hospital admission band on his arm that I snapped awake.

We sat for thirty or forty minutes in the lounge talking; conversation only pausing for me to refill his water glass in the kitchen, over and over again. I think we got to twelve.

Evidently one of the side effects of his antibiotics had been a dry mouth. Having had a dry mouth for four days in row, the number of shows he was doing under hot stage lights

---

[23] He's a consummate professional.

and then running from one venue to another carrying a guitar, Ashley hadn't really noticed that he had become dehydrated. He'd most likely not had a high enough fluid intake for two days. He had been drinking, but, how can I put this nicely, he's a big chap and was probably sweating out more than he realised.

Make sure you drink and eat enough while you're there.

PERSONAL EXPERIENCES FROM THE FRINGE

The 'Picnic' is the show I've produced the most at the Fringe. Since the first year in 2003 over twenty comics have taken part in it, with another twenty or so doing guest spots at some point. The biggest problem has always been getting the right personalities involved. The quality of someone's stand-up act is one thing, what people are like to work with is totally different. Some people are easier to work with than others and it's difficult to know before you go up there who is going to cause problems. These are all events and disagreements that have occurred over the nine years I've produced the show.

2003

EGOS

Waiting outside the venue one day with two performers from the show, the two other performers from the show that week phoned up on their third day and declared that, *"acts of their quality and standing should not have to go out flyering for a show they're in,"* therefore *"we're not going to go and do it."* Upon hearing this the immediate reaction from the two other acts with me was, if *"they're not going to go out and do it, then we're not going to go out and do it."*

We were in a paid venue in 2003 and if we didn't sell enough tickets I was financially responsible to the venue for any outstanding expenses. I hadn't had to pay anything up front for hiring the venue, but the deal was a fifty percent split of ticket money after expenses. Certain expenses still had to be met. Loss of revenue was a big problem.

I'm not sure I handled the situation brilliantly but after speaking to the two acts who were with me at the venue, I called the other two back and explained to them if they didn't turn up to do the flyering, then there was no point in them turning up to do the show. We'd simply do it without them. They arrived half an hour later and every day after that, but there was tension. The other two were convinced that they were only pretending to go out flyering.

LESSONS LEARNT

* When flyering it's best if everyone either goes out in pairs so they're all in sight of each other. Just because people are taking flyers out with them doesn't mean they are actually flyering. After one performer left one year we found a stock pile of flyers at another venue just piled up on a table.

* Performers need to invest in the show up front when the venue is booked and you need to have extra cash on hand for any unforeseen expenses. Once the Fringe is over getting money out of people is nearly impossible. In 2003 I was left with a £300 bill from the venue, divided by £30 each I was only able to recover about £90.

* It's best to have a written record of what everyone is agreeing to do in advance of the Fringe. Written agreements can be referred back to in the event of any disagreements or sketchy recollections. Email is the easiest way of doing this.

2004

This show was financed and organised differently. Everyone put £100 into a kitty to cover the upfront expenses of Fringe entry, advert in the Fringe guide and posters and flyers. We also did a number of preview shows around the North West and the money raised went into a fund towards a flat. Cast members from the 'Picnic' paid a reduced rate compared to the other occupants of the flat.

SOCIABLE DRINKERS

On the first day of the show one act turned up very drunk[24]. How he'd managed to get into the state he was in at 5:30pm was a mystery – even for Scotland. Either he'd really been going for it in the three hours since I'd last seen him when he was, *"just having a cheeky pint"* or he was the world's biggest lightweight. On stage his words were slurred, other people's material came out, then he wouldn't get off the stage when his time was done. He went on for nearly twenty minutes of a one hour show when he should have been doing around seven minutes. Consequently everyone else on the bill had to cut down their sets so the show finished on time. There was a £75 a minute fine in place for shows that overran. We had to finish on time! The rest of the show was difficult because the audience weren't impressed with what had happened at the beginning and no one comic had enough time to stay on long enough to win them around.

The following morning we had to sit down and have a chat. I explained that the audience would have been well within their rights to ask for a refund, which would have drawn the venue management staff's attention to the show. Clearly they wouldn't be happy if they thought the performers were compromising the show because they were drunk. They'd also not be very happy at losing revenue having to give out full refunds. I didn't want them to start thinking of us as a liability. Plus the other acts were also upset that they'd not had their allotted stage time. We came to an agreement that it didn't matter how drunk he got once we'd finished the show, beforehand he'd have to give it a rest.

---

[24] The first act in the shows history to do this, certainly not the last.

LACK OF TEAM WORK

In the same year in a different week we had a line up which was by far our strongest. We had a good format going and used the same compère, opening and closing act. One act was considerably better than everyone else and did a good job closing most days. We all thought we should stick with this format. Except for the act who was opening the show – he apparently didn't want to be opening – and to show his annoyance at doing the opening slot again on the final day, he very considerately went on and did the best jokes from everyone else's act.

EGOS AGAIN

Despite a written agreement of what everyone was going to get out of a week of doing the show, I received an email from one performer asking me to make arrangements "for any bookers from the big agencies and clubs, to come to the show in the week he was performing in it." Evidently booking a venue, getting a schedule of preview shows to finance the advertising, sorting out all promotional material for the show and arranging cut price accommodation wasn't enough. I was now in charge of their comedy career as well. When I spoke to them in October to ask for bank details in order to give them back their £100 plus profit, the same performer rather generously referred to the experience as, *"that rubbish waste of time."*

BOUNCING CHEQUES

The most significant event of 2004 was the company who programmed and ran my venue went into administration. Once the Fringe office did the final pay out at the beginning of October, I received my final figures from them and cheque for the sum of £135. However I learned shortly after that the bank weren't honouring a lot of the other cheques. Ours went through without a hitch, presumably due to it being such a small amount.

The following year I learned from someone that worked at the venue that they just didn't get enough punters through the door and had spent too much money setting up the venue, which was a shame because it was the only major venue in the city that was air conditioned.

LESSONS LEARNT

* When performers are only at the Fringe for a week they often treat it as a holiday rather than work. Depending on the time of day they can regularly turn up after they've had a few or still hungover from the night before.

* Another favourite argument over the years are the acts that don't show up for the photo shoot for the poster, and then complain that they aren't on the poster.

2005

In 2005 we moved to a free venue on the Royal Mile, The Canons Gait. We kept the £100 up front system despite the fact we had lower overheads. The extra cash on hand was used to pay a deposit for the flat.

Again another flat mate lost the plot part way through. Dave Smith was supposed to be sharing a room with someone else but he started locking the door and not allowing his room-mate in. He'd also become more withdrawn and had noticeably stopped bathing. His room-mate eventually gave up on sharing the room and took to sleeping in the lounge as the body odour smell became too much to deal with.

A four star review came out for our show. On the day it was published, upon learning of the review, Dave became fixated on the idea that the show had been reviewed. He wanted to know what it said and whether or not he was mentioned. He was so fixated on the review, five minutes into his stand-up set he decided he couldn't wait to read the review any longer and abruptly told the audience he was off. He walked straight out of the venue and went looking for a copy of 'ThreeWeeks.' What he would have done if the show he'd walked out of had been reviewed I have no idea.

In subsequent years I've also heard other people talk about Dave going mental again part way through and hearing people joke that you set your Fringe clock by one of his breakdowns.

A CAD AND A BOUNDER

You hear many stories at the Fringe, a good one from 2005 was Alan Smith. For most of the time during the festival when I'd spoken to Alan he seemed obsessed by how much money our show had got in its collection. It was the first thing he asked me when I bumped into him. Before the final weekend of the festival he disappeared and no one knew where he was. One bar manager was getting a bit worried because he'd been running up a tab at her bar and she'd also discovered he'd been using their account with the local taxi firm without their knowledge. The account was used as a way of making sure the female bar staff got safely home late at night. Alan had evidently been getting taxis all over the city and charging it to the bar.

His flatmates had the answer. He'd done a moonlight flit on the final Friday of the festival owing them rent money; he'd apparently been borrowing money from other people too.

Alan was always with a young woman when I saw him and I assumed that she was his girlfriend. An assumption that was correct when we found out his wife had been back in London the whole time.

LESSONS LEARNT

* You need two bathrooms if you've got eight people in a

flat.

* VIP only bars might occasionally have the odd film star knocking around or former Labour MPs drinking champagne with their entourage but they are exceptionally boring places. It's more fun hanging around with your mates.

2006

The population of Edinburgh rises from approximately 500,000 to a million people during the Fringe. Yet despite this increase in some ways it remains a small place. You bump into nearly every comic you've ever gigged with in the street. You know all the gossip and what everyone is up to.

Dave Turquoise had a few drinks one night which is quite normal for someone visiting the city. The following morning, feeling a little bit delicate yet claiming to only be suffering a mild hangover, Turquoise and Bob Darwin went to get some breakfast in the City Restaurant, a café located next to the Festival Theatre. Shortly after finishing his meal, Dave started to feel that maybe their maxi sized breakfast might not have been the wisest choice he'd ever made. Starting to feel that the mild hangover was actually bigger than he'd first given it credit for, he had to run to the toilets where he projectile vomited £4.99 worth of food.

What was probably only seconds later I was standing in my flat when I got a text message from Bob Darwin which read, "Yes, yes, comedy gold, Turkey's just spewed in the City Restaurant." Being fairly amused by this idea I forwarded the message to Seymour Mace who was standing on the Royal Mile talking to comedy agent Ashley Boroda. Seymour read out the text when he received it and then he and Ashley parted company. Ashley walked from the Royal Mile, along North Bridge and reached the City Restaurant at the exact moment a paler than normal looking Turquoise emerged. He was left looking confused too when Ashley asked him, "did you just spew up in there?"

MORE RANDOM THAN YOU'RE EXPECTING

In my final 'Butterfly Effect' performance a random nutter walked in twenty minutes into the show and started throwing wet underpants at some people in the crowd. Obviously that fitted in with the chaos theory theme quite nicely but was a bit distracting. The problem with the Fringe is that the odd and weird happens all the time. It's hard to know if that audience realised that was something genuinely happening or something they thought I'd set up myself as part of the show.

LESSONS LEARNT

* You need to have at least a ninety minute break between performing in shows. I was doing an hour in 'The Butterfly Effect' followed by a twenty minute set in the 'Picnic.' I only had about forty five minutes between the shows, so still felt tired when the second show started.

* You need to work out a meal schedule around your shows. If you don't have enough food in you before a show, you don't have enough energy. Eat too close to show time and you don't have enough energy as your body is trying to digest your meal.

* If you're in a flat with seven other people make sure you have ear plugs and remember to put your phone on silent before you go to bed. Stops you being disturbed by any late night drinkers who can't find their keys and you get to listen to some great voice mails in the morning that start with, *"I can't get in...."*

2007

THE IVAN HOE

Due to the ongoing and very public disagreement at the time between Peter Buckley-Hill and the Laughing Horse over the future of free shows at the Fringe, we had to move from our planned venue. A friend – who was also looking for a suitable space to perform a solo show in – and I decided to drive up to Edinburgh one Saturday afternoon to have a first-hand look at some of the spaces on offer. One venue, The Ivan Hoe, located just off Princes Street – the main shopping street in Edinburgh – seemed ideal. From the venue diagram it appeared to have good sight lines and be located in a basement room away from the main bar. On entering the room the first thing we noticed was the overwhelming food smell coming out of the kitchen. The kitchen was evidently located downstairs next to the stage area. We felt that the smell was quite distracting and the potential noise from the kitchen meant it was not an ideal space to perform in. My friend politely declined the venue, which very definitely turned out to have been the right decision. In between the deadline for shows being listed with the Fringe office in April and July, The Ivan Hoe closed down. All shows programmed to be in there had to find an alternate location. This effectively meant their Fringe programme entries were useless as they were advertising the show as being on in venue that no longer existed. The Fringe office were, however, able to update the shows location on edfringe.com and in newspaper listings as well as the ticket office.

To make matters worse for the performers who had been relocated, they discovered their new venue was quite far away from other Fringe venues and that they were no longer performing in a separate room from the main bar. The new space was in the corner of a busy pub. Aside from this being very noisy the bar had a lot of regulars who having seen the shows on offer in the first few days were already bored by them and had proceeded to constantly interrupt and heckle the performers. By the second week of the Fringe a number of the shows in the venue simply decided to cut their losses and go home.

On 27th August 2007, a review of Owen Niblock's show citied the fact the show had been moved from the bar to a third venue – a café upstairs – so the bar could host a concert from Scottish one hit wonders Stiltskin.

WHEN STORIES ARE TOO PERSONAL

In 2006 a friend of mine – and most of the 'Picnic' cast – was diagnosed with testicular cancer. He went through hell in 2006 but thankfully by the beginning of 2007 he was back in good health and had decided he was going to put on a show about his experience.

Unfortunately he just wasn't ready to talk about what had clearly been an horrific experience. He performed one show at a Free Festival venue to a small, and by all accounts fairly disinterested, crowd. The finishing touch, as far as he was concerned, was an audience member who got up part way through the show for a smoke at the back of the room.

He left Edinburgh approximately forty hours after he arrived and to this day I don't think has ever performed again. Some things are just too personal to talk about.

ONE HOUR IS BEST

In 2007 we had the idea of doing the 'Picnic' in an hour and a half slot. We intended to include an interval in the show. It didn't work. At the forty five minute mark when we called an interval the audience would just leave. We had to shift the show back to an hour long format meaning the venue space was empty for about forty five minutes before the next show started.

BACKSTAGE BRAVADO

Comedians aren't always the best judge of what is in bad taste when they're left alone with other comics. Dave Turquoise is the epitome of this. Waiting in the back stage area before doing a short spot in the 'Picnic' he and another comic were messing around with a roll of black tape. Hitler moustaches were worn and a black tape swastika put on the back of Dave's jacket.

Dave's short spot didn't go well in the show and he sneaked out straight after and headed back in the direction of the flat to get out of the way.

Around seventy minutes later as I entered the lounge in the flat, I had a short conversation with Dave as he was on his way out. As he came to leave he picked up his jacket from the dining table and put it back on. Noticing the tape on the back of jacket I pointed it out to him. His eyes widened, he started to look paler than normal and went through a range of facial expressions similar to the scene at the end of 'The Usual Suspects'.

"****, I was in Tesco for fifteen minutes......I wondered why no one was standing behind me at that cash machine."

Evidently the people of Edinburgh had spotted a forty something white man with a shaved head wearing a swastika on his back and had decided to steer clear of him.

COMEDY IS A SERIOUS BUSINESS

In 2007, the compilation show 'The Big Value Comedy Show' wasn't having as successful a run as it had in the past. Part way through the Fringe a meeting was called for all the acts, managers, agents and promoters to see what strategies could be used to drum up trade. One of the performers from that year, David Longley, describes how the meeting went.

"Everyone had been invited to the meeting. It was very tense, and very serious. I decided I wouldn't talk to anyone unless it was through a toilet roll tube. I made a series of points and suggestions, all spoken through the tube.

Part way through the meeting the promoter, who had become quite annoyed by that point, tried to grab it off me, shouting "are you going to say everything through that tube?" I put the tube to my mouth and said "yes."

It was only later on that the other acts realised that there hadn't been any toilet rolls in the room and concluded that Dave had specifically brought it to the meeting with him from home.

THE BIGGEST PROBLEM WITH ORGANISING GROUP SHOWS

This year's 'Picnic' was the fifth show that I had produced and it had a large cast of different comics each week. I felt I was under too much stress. My own show 'One Man Defective Story' was going badly and the 'Picnic' wasn't great either. Cast members were turning up and announcing that they were going home two days early or were ringing to say they were arriving a day later than they were supposed to leaving me to find last minute replacements.

In the shows that were happening, the cast members were turning up later and later each day. The room and equipment required setting up and if I didn't do it, it appeared that no one else would. I started to feel that organising such a large cast couldn't go on. Comics are lazy by nature and I got the feeling that I was expected to do everything for them.

Audience figures were down for the show and I became suspicious that only one or two of the cast were actually going out flyering or doing anything to promote the show.

This was the first show where everyone didn't get their initial £100 investment back.

LESSONS LEARNT

* There is no substitute for actually seeing a venue beforehand rather than just relying on diagrams and photographs.

* The buildings used by the paid venues have a full time use the rest of the year and are leased by the venues for the August period, which means there is little chance of them going broke before the Fringe starts. However free shows tend to be located in bars that are open all year around and therefore there is the possibility of them closing before the Fringe starts. Seeing how busy they are the rest of year is a good indicator of their overall financial state. As is checking the fridges behind the bar. Bars usually keep fridges well stocked, a bar with empty fridges is a possible indication that they don't have enough cash on hand to buy any stock or their suppliers have withdrawn their line of credit.

* Trying to perform and produce three shows is too many; we also scheduled a late night comedy show intended to be different from the earlier show with different material and more unusual acts. It ended up as the same acts and the same material and lost more money than the 'Picnic.'

* It's really a team effort and if you can't work together, it's going to go wrong.

* Keep it simple. Organising the show each day shouldn't be so complex that the performances suffer.

2008

My favourite year for the 'Picnic.' Working with people who are reliable and committed to the project and able to foresee problems or solve them as they happen makes things so much easier. I found the entire experience enjoyable and didn't feel any pressure at all. I also think it was the first year in history that nobody went mental in our flat. With no other shows to work on I was more focussed on writing new stand-up material and able to drop in some new stuff each day.

ACCOMMODATION ISSUES AGAIN

There was never any love lost between me and the landlord of our flat, mainly because every time it came to handing the keys back over she was never around. She'd be on holiday – no prizes for guessing who had just paid for that – and whoever she charged with the task of checking us out always complained the place wasn't clean and tidy enough. It was usually cleaner and tidier than it had been when we arrived and they'd always pick up on a mark on a carpet or work surface that had been there in the flat when we arrived. The day she rang up to ask me if I'd cancel one of my shows to let in the boiler repair man, I did think, "maybe it's time to move on." I personally think when you've paid someone £3600 that they can put themselves out a little bit when things aren't working. We all shared that feeling when she contacted us in 2009 to see if we wanted to rent the place again but told us she'd have to increase the rent, despite the fact the flat didn't have anywhere near the features other people's flats had, like a washing machine or internet access.

2009

MONEY AGAIN

The issue of performers not investing in shows arose again in 2009 when a friend of mine was doing a show with a student – James. Being a student, James didn't have the money to put into the shared show, as he had already paid for another show. My friend came to the Fringe to start the joint venture in week two after James had already been there with the other show for a week.

Problems started appearing pretty quickly. Audience numbers were low and the performance wasn't gelling. James clearly wasn't interested in flyering and had lost faith in the whole show. On one occasion James called off the show as he felt ill and on another he gave up on the performance part way through because the audience wasn't going with it leaving his co-performer to finish the show single-handedly with about thirty minutes to go.

After a few days things got back on track but their problems could have been predicted and they stemmed from a few obvious causes. If you're doing a show together you need to be equally invested. It helps if this is financial, but it's even more important for it to be a shared goal and commitment. They eventually had some good shows once they'd worked through their issues.

2010

AN AWARD WINNING PLAY

My relationship with people flyering for shows has always been a bit troubled. In 2003 myself and another act from the 'Picnic' nearly got into a fist fight with some drama students. One of them was inside a large cardboard box and would frequently get in front of people and drop to the floor to stop them from getting past until they took a flyer from one of his friends. After watching him do this to a guy trying to push someone in a wheel chair uphill, he then did it again to a young woman trying to get uphill with a push chair, whilst also carrying a lot of heavy shopping; she didn't actually have a free hand to take a flyer. My friend and I went and sat on the box so as he couldn't move. When the box started giving way and it looked like the guy inside was going to get crushed some of his friends tried to appear 'hard.' Unfortunately their drama skills weren't at a sufficient level for that to look convincing. My friend on the other hand was of a physical build and look that did not require any acting skills to appear convincing when he instructed them where to go.

In 2006 a few of us started asking overly pushy flyerers questions, such as, "is there any juggling in it?" When they'd say "no," we'd look disappointed and say, "but I like juggling." Occasionally when they thought there was the potential for them to sell a ticket they'd reply with, "well, there's a bit of juggling in it." As the festival went on juggling was switched to something else – nudity, racism, sandwiches. It was really uncomfortable when one of the 'Picnic' crew asked someone from a church group, "is there any bumming in it?"

In 2010 I got into one of those arguments that I apparently have a reputation for getting in. I was on the Royal Mile and a flyerer tried to hand me a flyer for, "*an award winning play.*" Looking at the flyer I couldn't see any mention of an award, so out of curiosity I asked what award had it won. He told me it was a "D*rama Award from BBC Manchester.*" Now I'd never heard of any drama awards at BBC Manchester and I was in there quite a lot in 2007 when I did 'The Butterfly Effect' pilot. So I asked him, "are you sure because I've never heard of them doing drama awards at BBC Manchester, what award did it win?" "Best play," was apparently the award. So I asked, any particular category? Apparently it was "*just best play,*" and when I asked when did it win this award? The answer was "*recently.*"

Now I'm told the moment I took my phone out and googled the name of the play and "award," was the moment I'd taken it too far. I'm not hundred percent sure that was the moment it went too far. Clearly the bit when I rang up someone who worked in the Drama Department at BBC Manchester was taking it too far. However in my defence they'd never heard of the play, writer or an award.

The following day I was back on the mile, when someone thrust a flyer in front of me and said *"award winning play,"* then after they'd noticed who they'd offered it to they turned and walked off.

UNCOMFORTABLE BEYOND BELIEF

Both myself and Ashley got into one of those conversations at our venue one day that neither of us could quite believe. People frequently come up and ask if they can have a spot in your show, but this guy didn't want a spot for himself he wanted a spot for his twelve year old son. Now we normally don't let kids in the audience, so we've certainly never considered letting one in the show. We tried to explain we just didn't have other comics in the show and in any case there was no way we'd put on someone we'd never seen before, regardless of age. To try and persuade us he told us the kid had *"some really good jokes about paedophiles,"* which again we explained wasn't really selling it to us. Eventually he left, clearly not happy.

A couple of days later a one star review turned up on Chortle for a show in another free venue. It started off explaining that the show might well have received a two star review were it not for the fact the person had employed a twelve year old boy as a warm up act. The reviewer described it as, *"the most appallingly inappropriate performance you could imagine,"* and that the word 'excruciating' did not come anywhere near describing how uncomfortable he'd felt watching the show as the boy's five minute set consisted of nothing but jokes about paedophilia.

In 2011, myself and Ashley were standing outside our venue flyering when a man came up and said, *"you remember me? You wouldn't let my kid do a spot in your show, any chance of a gig this year?"*

EVERYONE LOVES A CAR WRECK

A friend went in to watch a sketch show in one of the free venues. It was so bad he decided to leave after ten minutes and go for a quiet drink at the bar. When he came to leave the venue he had to walk past the room the show was in so out of curiosity he sneaked a peak at the room to see how the show was going. Evidently all audience members had walked out on the show but the performers were still going – playing to no one. Word soon got around among a lot of comics who started to go and watch the show just to see how bad it was.

2011

NO IDEA HOW IT WORKS

Late one night I turned up to do a compilation show and was introduced to some of the other acts whilst we were waiting for the show to start. When one of the acts learned I was doing a solo show she started asking me if she could have a ten minute spot in it. I tried explaining that it wasn't that kind of show. It was just me and a lot of material that I'd spent a year writing, she became quite offended and said, *"yes I understand that part, but it's an hour long show and I think doing that much time on your own is just greedy, you should give someone else a chance."*

ONE FLYER TOO MANY

A lot of the agencies hire students to do their flyering for them. Most likely recruited from the same universities they run gigs in the rest of the year. The Stand comedy club make sure that the people flyering have seen the shows they're flyering for. They're much more effective at selling your show if they know something about it, and you.

One year I was approached by someone flyering for Sarah Millican who told me she was a fantastic *"character comedian."* John Bishop once told me he'd been on the Royal Mile and been approached by someone who offered him a flyer for his own show. I can't imagine either of those flyering staff were actually getting anyone in for those shows.

I was on the Royal Mile taking photos one day when a student offered me a flyer for a show a comic I knew was doing. I was about to just smile and take the flyer, when she told me he was, *"an award winning comedian."* Out of curiosity I asked her which award he'd won – I knew he hadn't won anything. She told me that was what she'd been told to tell people. Jokingly I asked her if she'd seen the show and she sighed and said, *"yes...........I hated it, I just feel like such a horrible person telling people to go and see it, it's awful."* I wasn't really expecting that response; I felt as though I'd just accidentally broken someone's spirit. I gave her the phone numbers for a couple of different agencies I knew that employed flyerers at the Fringe, said try them they might well need staff. I also said that most of the shows they were promoting were actually quite good.

The following day I was having dinner with some friends and the comic whose show it was came in and joined us. The subject of his flyering team came up in conversation – I'd told everyone the story already. He told us he had three people flyering for him, *"two are all right but one's going to have to go, she's not getting anyone in."* In retrospect I wish I'd asked if the other two had seen his show.

YOU NEVER KNOW WHO'S IN THE CROWD

In the final part of my show 'Ian Fox Exposes Himself' I included a live action version of 'Where's Wally.' I'd persuaded Seymour Mace to dress up as Wally and I took pictures of him hidden in crowds around Manchester – in itself that was an experience neither of us are keen to repeat.

On the 10th August one guy in the crowd was spotting Wally a lot faster than everyone else, he got the first seven in a row. That's when he told us he worked for the publishing company that makes the book and had the business card to prove it. He was good!

FINANCIAL PROBLEMS

In December 2011 The Scotsman newspaper reported that the company Remarkable Arts, operator of one Fringe venue, had collapsed, failing to hand over box office takings to the theatre groups who had performed with them that year. Sadly a similar situation to the company I worked with in 2004.

BOB'S BOOKSHOP

Bob's Bookshop was a pop-up venue that appeared in an empty shop unit at the 2013 Fringe. The retail business previously in there closed down at the end of June and Bob Slayer was able to rent the premises for one month and use it as a venue – much to the annoyance of the neighbours. He was also using the basement as his own personal living quarters.

Bob's Bookshop was one of the most successful pop-up venues I've seen. Located on South College Street – a popular walking route between the Pleasance and Gilded Balloon – the curiosity value of the space, it's prime location and programming choice were the key to it's success. One show in particular made the venue more conspicuous, 'The Half Naked Chef' – dressed only in y-fronts, chef's hat and apron – incorporated activity on the street into his show. Audience seating had been repositioned so as they looked out on to the street and he would frequently leave the stage area to grab passers-by and involve them in the show – whether they wanted to or not. Walking past in the evening you would quite often see; home-made sold notices attached to vans parked on the street, melons speared on railings, chairs from the venue in the gutter labelled "the naughty seats" and the chef on his hands and knees in the street smashing an onion with a hammer. You'd also hear a large amount of laughter going on inside the bookshop.

Bob didn't manage to repeat the magic in 2014 with a similar venue but in 2015 he bought a bus!

WHAT DO THE AUDIENCE THINK?

One year, in September, after returning home from a month at the Fringe, I went out for a drink with my friend Rob who has been to the Fringe but not for about ten years – I imagine it was quite different back then as I've noticed it changing over the years. A friend of his came over to talk to us and during the conversation it came up I'd just come back from the Fringe. This guy said he'd never been before, always wanted to go, and asked what's it like? Before I had chance to say anything Rob answered him, "it's all right, but after a while you do think to yourself, the cream of the comedy crop is at this festival and yet somehow I've ended up sitting here watching this ****!"

CONCLUSIONS

HAVE A SHOW

That might seem obvious but it's surprising how many people book a slot in January with no idea of what they'll be doing in August. If you're a new comedian and you regularly do 10 minute slots don't sign up for a full hour thinking that you can set yourself the challenge of having an hour of material by August. Over the last few years I've seen loads of new acts try and fail at this, mainly because putting together an hour is extremely difficult: forty minutes is hard enough but it's that last twenty where it really goes wrong.

Instead, the best thing to do is find some other comics in a similar position and put on a showcase where you do 10-15 minutes each and rotate as headliner and compère. There are enormous advantages to doing this. Firstly you get all the benefits of performing every day, such as, increased confidence and becoming more relaxed and loose on stage without the downside of having to endure the painful sight of audience members getting up and walking out on you. Also you don't get a mauling from whatever press turns up to see you and it's much cheaper as you split the costs between you. Finally, any press reviews you pick up will be likely to be positive – unless you're completely rubbish – and you'll come out of it with one or two decent quotes for your CV.

Also, and this is worth considering, showcases keep you out of the running for the 'Edinburgh Comedy Award'. You're eligible for the newcomer award if you're doing your first solo show of over fifty minutes in length, which means that if you've been in compilations you're still considered a newcomer down the line. Successful examples of this strategy include Sarah Millican who did 'The Big Value Comedy Show' in 2006 before doing her own show in 2008 and winning best newcomer, Josie Long who also did 'Big Value' and then a double header the year later where she did thirty minutes, before doing her solo show in 2006 and winning best newcomer and the star of the 2010 Free Festival Imran Yusuf, who in previous years compered the 'Laughing Horse Pick of the Fringe' shows before being nominated for best newcomer. Each of these guys went up to Edinburgh in showcases to see how it works for themselves before jumping in with both feet.

One final thing on this point. Showcases really are a good starting point. The first year I came up I produced a show with about twelve other comedians in it, some of whom have gone on to star in films and sitcoms and become circuit regulars. We had a great time while we were up there doing shows and it felt like we were part of something. It's a time I look back on fondly. We had a guest headliner in our shows which varied each day just to give the show a good finish. During 2003 and 2004 they included Alan Carr, Jason Manford, Mick Ferry, Anvil Springstein, Alfie Joey and Seymour Mace. Great acts will often happily do guest spots as it's a good way for them to promote their own show. If you're a new act, I definitely recommend this strategy. It's low risk and you may even get a story out of it. In 2011, the organiser of one showcase, when his guest act hadn't showed up, wandered out on the street, correctly assumed the person walking past the venue he sort of recognised was a comic and successfully press-ganged them into filling the headline spot. He now remembers that as the day that Stewart Lee headlined his show.

LIFE AFTER THE FRINGE

Some of the most successful shows that go up there aren't the ones that win awards. This is worth considering when you plan out your show. In 2003 Mike Gunn did a show at the Pleasance Dome called 'Mike Gunn: Uncut'. It was true life account of years spent as a drug addict and the slow recovery process. It was dark, funny and poignant. It didn't get nominated for any awards but since then Mike has been paid to perform the show around the country in prisons and schools. In terms of financial success, he's still reaping the benefit of something he did nine years before.

In 2006 Toby Hadoke's show 'Moths Ate My Doctor Who Scarf' went on to become a BBC7 two part show, toured in comedy venues up and down the country, returned to the Fringe for a short run in 2007 and for a sell-out show at the EICC in 2010 and is still in demand at science fiction conventions.

In 2007 I was commissioned by the BBC to write a radio pilot based on 'The Butterfly Effect.' The process started around the end of September 2006, I went in to meet a producer at the BBC in Manchester who had recently taken on the job of producing comedy shows. It was an informal meeting in the bar over coffee. I simply told him about my show – he liked the idea as it stuck out from the usual submissions he got on regular basis for "a sketch show with a large number of funny train announcements" – and we discussed how we could go about doing it on the radio. I thought the chimp story was the most likely bit to use, a narrator to tell the story with the scenes acted out like sketches. One cast of four actors would play nineteen characters. Months of meetings, discussion and refinement of the treatments followed and in May 2007 we recorded the fifteen minute pilot based on a script written by myself and Carl Cooper. Each week it would be a different story with different chain reactions. Some taking thousands of years. The show wasn't picked up as a series and lies in the vaults of the BBC somewhere, although I still think of it as a great achievement for a show that only cost £350 to put on.

CLOSING POINTS

Draw your own conclusions and take from this collection of advice and stories what you need. The many times I've been asked questions over coffee by people who want to go up and do a show, these are the points I usually make at the end of our conversation.

* If you've never been to the Fringe before I would recommend that for the first year you go up you just try to get as many gigs as possible, rather than jumping in head-first with your own show. Until you've experienced what it's like I don't think you can plan effectively. You need an image of the Fringe in your mind's eye. You also need to see as many shows as possible by experienced acts to get an idea of how they work the space and use the time slot.

* For your first show a compilation is much more manageable than a solo hour. That said, you need to

carefully choose the people you work with. Spend some time getting to know them outside of gigs. If you're going to share a flat or work with someone for a month, day in, day out, then you need to know that you can get on with each other.

* Before risking a massive amount of money I'd suggest that you look into doing a free show for your first time, with a view to moving up to paid venues down the line. Comedy award nominees 'Pappy's Funny Club' did their first show in a free venue, their second in a mid-price venue and third in a premium space.

* Be realistic in your expectations. Achieving fame and fortune in three weeks in August is in all probability very unlikely. Set more attainable goals, like a little bit of decent press, fifty or so extra gigs to improve your skills or the refinement of material you've been working on – I know one comedian who effectively thinks of each year's Fringe show as a new draft, and something that they improve each time. Making new friends, making new contacts, or just enjoying yourself, these are all achievable and worthwhile goals.

* When it's over, go! Don't hang about too long afterwards. The site of the Fringe gates being brought down and all the venues without posters and locked up is quite depressing. There is a post Fringe come down period so I'd recommend making sure you've got stuff in your diary for September once you've had a suitable rest.

* Make sure your partners and spouses realise what you're doing up in Edinburgh and that you're up there working, not just on a long holiday. A lot of relationships suffer tension if your partner thinks you're just avoiding them for a month.

FINAL WORD

I would not have written this book if I didn't think that the Fringe was worth investing time and money into. Over the last few years I've invested the equivalent of a year of my life working on Fringe shows and I've found it very rewarding.

I hope that the benefit of my experience will help you do your own show at the Fringe and increase your chances of getting the most out of it.

This is the third edition of this book and the plan is to update it every few years. As you've bought this book it seems unfair to charge you for a small update so check the site

http://theianfox.wordpress.com for new additions to this text.

Ian Fox, 2016

USEFUL RESOURCES

If you're on Facebook search for the group Edinburgh Fringe Performers Forum. It's a helpful place that I helped set up and run for performers to ask questions and help each other out. In previous years there has been helpful threads with accommodation being advertised, gigs being offered and great printing deals. Plus during the Fringe helpful things going on, such as, lost iPads being reunited with owners, discussions on best bus tickets to get, and my personal favourite, where to get the best spray tan in Edinburgh.

APPENDIX 1: PRODUCTION SCHEDULE FOR THE 2017 FRINGE

JANUARY TO MARCH

* Book a venue.

MARCH

* Approximately three weeks before the final deadline for listing a show is the discount deadline. This is a saving of nearly a hundred pounds. Better to save the money now and make better use of it whilst you're in Edinburgh. Once a show is registered you can still make adjustments to your forty word blurb and change artwork up to a week after the final deadline for show submissions.

APRIL

* Final deadline for listing in the Fringe programme.

APRIL TO MAY

* Find somewhere to live for the month. Now this is a stressful one! Ringing up estate agents and trying not to get ripped off or ending up with a place in the middle of nowhere. However to make life easier if you're on Facebook you can join the group Edinburgh Fringe Performers Forum and look for the accommodation thread where performers are both looking for and advertising available accommodation.

* Start looking for cheap train or plane tickets to Edinburgh.

MAY TO JUNE

* Write a full press release so it is ready when the Fringe programme comes out.

* Prepare websites and any additional material, such as, YouTube videos to seduce audiences into your show, again so they're online when the programme is published.

* Order promotional material for your show, such as, T-shirts and hoodies. The cheap deals usually have a long print delivery time as the merchandise makes it way from Eastern Europe.

* Start previewing your show so when you reach Edinburgh it's ready for the spotlight.

JUNE

* Fringe programme is published. Fringe box office tickets go live.

* Start approaching publications for publicity. Include press release and any web links and videos etc.

* Last chance to order back-up cables and devices for your show box. Allowing 3 weeks delivery time.

JULY

* Prepare poster and flyer artwork files to go to the printers. Schedule delivery for about a week before you arrive. Too early and it might get put into storage and forgotten about. Too late and it might not get put up in time. Check with the venue when they want to receive stuff. Posters and flyers need to arrive before you do.

FESTIVAL DATES

Dates for the festival change each year. The Fringe closes on the August bank holiday Monday in England – not Scotland.

MONDAY 31ST JULY: Venues start technical rehearsals which carry on until the first shows start. Venues won't be open to the public during these times.

TUESDAY 1ST AUGUST: The day most acts will travel to Edinburgh. The most likely day to bump into comedy's superstars at motorway services and train stations.

WEDNESDAY 2ND AUGUST: Preview shows start in the Pleasance and Gilded Balloon plus press launches for other venues.

THURSDAY 3RD AUGUST: Preview shows at Assembly, Underbelly and The Stand. Free Festival shows also start.

FRIDAY 4TH AUGUST: The Fringe officially begins

SATURDAY 5TH AUGUST: Start of PBH Free Fringe shows.

There then follows three weeks of mayhem.

TUESDAY 15TH AUGUST: Usually the day most acts choose for their day off. Typically a slow day for ticket sales and approximately the half-way point.

SATURDAY 26TH AUGUST: Some PBH Free Fringe shows close.

SUNDAY 27TH AUGUST: Shows at the Caves, The Stand and Free Festival close.

MONDAY 28TH AUGUST: Final shows at Pleasance and Gilded Balloon. Closing Party at The Stand. Last 'Late'N'Live' at the Gilded Balloon. Performers start to go home, as they only rented accommodation for 28 days.

OCTOBER

Fringe box office usually pays out at the end of September, so early in October you'll either receive your payout from your venue or an invoice.

APPENDIX 2: ILLUSTRATIONS

Illustration 1: Poster using black bar design

APPENDIX 2: ILLUSTRATIONS

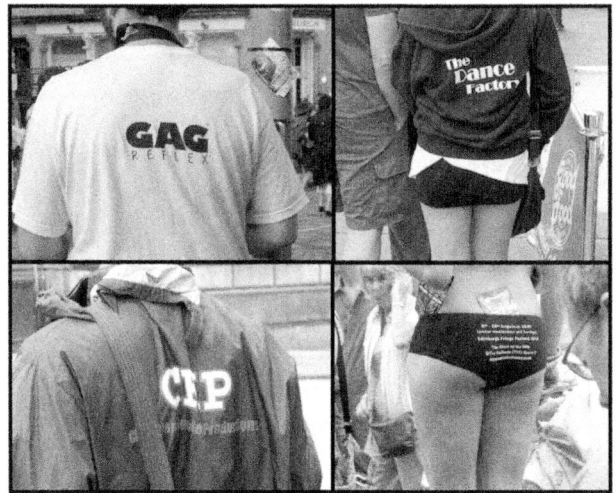

Illustration 2: Range of promotional items.

Printed in Great Britain
by Amazon